CW00421186

The Meeting

ELSBETH LINDNER

Harbour

First published in 2023 by Harbour Books (East) Ltd
P O Box 10594, Chelmsford, Essex CM1 9PB
info@harbourbooks.co.uk

Copyright © Elsbeth Lindner 2023

The moral right of the author has been asserted

All rights reserved. No part of this publication may be reproduced in any
form or by any means without the prior written permission of the publisher

Every effort has been made to trace copyright holders and to obtain their
permission for the use of copyright material. The publisher apologises
for any errors or omissions and would be grateful to be notified of any
corrections that should be incorporated in future editions

A catalogue record of this book is available from the British Library

ISBN 9781905128358

Typeset by Tetragon, London
Printed and bound in Great Britain by Clays Ltd, Elcograf S.p.A

Contents

I dedicate this book to all of them, the Lindners, the Levys, the Bornsteins, all the family branches and individuals: those who suffered; those who survived; the ones I knew and the ones I never met. They are an indissoluble part of me.

This book began as a wish to accumulate, in one place, as much knowledge, memory and sense of character as might still be available about an intriguing relative. The work started at, or perhaps later than, the eleventh hour, the key players being long deceased. There were surprises near the surface, while other facts remained stubbornly unavailable. Meanwhile, the project expanded in multiple directions.

Collecting and assembling the scraps, speaking to those who remembered, delving into the files and reading the letters has been a curious but satisfying mission. And having the tirelessly generous companionship of Lee Hemphill on this journey was part of the enrichment it brought.

I

The Meeting

EVEN on the finest day in England, Stoke-on-Trent is scarcely a pretty place. Famed as one of novelist Arnold Bennett's 'five towns', as the birthplace of aeronautical engineer R. J. Mitchell (designer of the World War II fighter the Spitfire), but best known for its pottery industry – Wedgwood, Spode – it retains to this day its grim Victorian aspect. The railway station, effectively a wind tunnel built of rust-red brick, looks little changed since the invention of the steam engine.

Here, in December 1967, a father and daughter wait with some excitement. Excepting a brief encounter in Paris in 1950, the father has not spent time with his brother since before World War II. The daughter, aged sixteen, has grown up in a family almost devoid of relatives beyond her parents and an older sister. There are no grandparents, no uncles or aunts barring the one on the incoming train. No other blood relations exist in the country. A few outliers live in Germany and Belgium, and there's one cousin, a concentration camp survivor, alive in Holland. But life has essentially been lived without extended family, shallowly rooted in the English Midlands.

When the train from London arrives, a slight, contained figure alights, carrying a single item of luggage. He is small and slim, bald with a fringe of dark hair around the back of the skull. A small black pipe is clenched between his teeth.

This was to be my first, indeed my only meeting with my uncle, Richard Lindner.

Richard was a figure of family myth and magic. In contrast with my own family – shopkeepers who, for random, half-comprehended reasons, happened to dwell in an obscure corner of Staffordshire – he was a star, the glory-boy living in New York, a painter who mingled with the famous and the bohemian, and seemed to be rich. Each Christmas, we would receive a large cardboard box of gifts selected by him from Bloomingdale's. One year a stupendous wooden sledge arrived, with curved runners and a slatted seat, superior in every measure to the local, home-made competition. More usually the boxes contained clothes whose quality and stylishness we would only come to appreciate in later years. But my mother would insist we wear them immediately anyway. One year, when I was perhaps ten, a striped shirtwaist arrived for my sister, an olive cotton shirt and tweed pencil skirt/waistcoat combination for me. Blackfriars Junior School had never seen the like. The mockery of my peers over this outfit, ridiculous on my pudgy, pre-teen body, haunts me still.

There were hats too – real fur bonnets, or rainbow-knitted Tibetan pull-ons with ear flaps and plaited tassels. And for my parents, *objets* from far-flung places. I remember a Mexican horse and rider, made of coloured woven straw; a huge, heavy brass brazier from India; a Fornasetti ashtray; a Central American rug woven in shades of caramel and scarlet; a circular Spanish candelabrum of contorted black metal. These parcels and their eclectic contents arrived as if from a glossy parallel universe of culture and taste.

Some of Richard's early or associated art dotted our home, notably a large watercolour of Offenbach conducting an orchestra, with a vista of whiskered and bonneted bourgeois audience faces ranged behind him. This hung over the living-room sofa and was pointed out proudly to Richard when he arrived. But the artist was dismissive. 'I've painted hundreds of those,' he commented.

In the dining room, there was a framed pencil miniature of Richard, complete with pipe and scribble of hair, as well as a gorgeous post-Impressionist watercolour of women skipping in a tropical landscape. This painting, signed by the Dutch artist Campendonk, had, according to family lore – let's call this stream of information the apocrypha; there will be more to come – been the result of an artists' swap: a picture by the Dutchman for one of Richard's. My father had apparently admired the Dutch work so much that his brother had passed it on as a gift.

Upstairs, my parents kept an oblong, gold and blue tin box containing the clutch of family scraps, photos and documents that had survived their separate journeys when fleeing Nazi Germany in 1939. Alongside was a tattered roll of posters advertising pianos manufactured by a British company, Barnes. As a pre-war commercial artist, Richard had painted their luscious watercolour illustrations in 1936. There were also some books he had illustrated – *Grock: Life's a Lark* (Heinemann, 1931); *Madame Bovary* (Peter Pauper Press, 1944) – and some of the original pencil illustrations.

And my parents had begun to compile a scrapbook illustrating his rise, after the 1950s, as a full-time creative artist. It contained newspaper cuttings about his distinctive figurative art featuring monumental men and women in bold colours. His most famous painting, *The Meeting*, was now in the possession of New York's Museum of Modern Art (MoMA). It featured family members, friends of Richard's and symbolic figures – a cat, King Ludwig II of Bavaria, a corseted female – each of which was totemic.

To me, though, most significant of all was the news that had arrived earlier in that year of 1967, that his gloomy face was included among the notables on the cover of the Beatles' groundbreaking new album, *Sergeant Pepper's Lonely Hearts*

Club Band. As far as I was concerned, this was both thrilling and confirmatory. Everything I had ever suspected about being different – a central component of myself, then and now – was hereby celebrated. Otherness – even better, *Jewish* otherness – could equate to exceptionalism. Richard Lindner knew the Beatles (or so it seemed). He visibly ranked alongside Marlon Brando, Marilyn Monroe and Karl Marx.

So, the arrival of Richard in Stoke-on-Trent was a momentous event, the advent of an idol.

What do I remember of his visit now, more than fifty years later? Less, of course, than I would like. There were his clothes, understated but clearly expensive and stylish: the double-denim jeans and jacket, the suede shirt. There was his insistence on smoking his pipe at the dinner table, both between and during courses, despite my mother's expressed displeasure.

There were the humour and indulgence of his time spent with me – less so my sister, who was immersed in her engagement, to be announced that Christmas – which reached their peak on one indelible evening, with him sitting on the above-mentioned sofa, drawing swift sketches of the boys who lay in my future. One sported a beard, one had long, shaggy hair (yes, I met both of them, and some of the others he imagined, too). To my everlasting regret, these sketches are now lost.

But the pair of crayon sketches he drew for my mother and me – mine a typical Lindner moll with alarming lips and breasts, my mother's a gangster in a trilby, garnished with the phrase 'Forgive me my dear Else' (what for? the smoking? the lifelong family disagreements?) – are hanging in my own home today.

Also indelible is the memory of the bad blood between the two brothers that predictably surfaced before the brief visit was over. Richard, the older of the two, did not share my father Arthur's view of their parents. Arthur had idolized both his father Julius and his mother Mina. They were, according to him, role models, loving and deeply caring. (Such photographs of them that exist don't contradict this view, my grandparents' faces expressing a kind of gentle restraint. Admittedly, some of these were taken by Arthur, who, at one point in a peripatetic history, was a photographer with a studio in pre-war Paris.)

Richard's opinion was less sunny. By his account, Julius was 'a nice man whom I loved, but he was a coward. He shifted responsibility for everything onto my mother and that made her an imposing figure... She wasn't very intelligent, a very Wagnerian woman, physically too – with a bust!'[1]

In an article in the *World Journal Tribune* from 1967, he expanded on Mina:

> After all these years, I am still trying to discover the riddle of my mother. She has been dead for years, but I never understood her. I think I'm beginning to now. My mother was American. She went to Germany when she was 20 years old... Her obsession was to become as European as possible. And she failed. As a child, I found her behavior almost grotesque. What I mean is, she could never quite reconcile her enormous desire for being a true European mother with her strong Puritanical temperament. The harder she tried, the more bizarre it became. And I became more and more confused as to what she expected of me.[2]

Puritanical, bourgeois and strict. This had all grated on Richard, as did his parents' insistence on family visits, every Sunday, to the grave of the boys' dead sister Lizzy. Richard, for whom Lizzy's death had been a seismic loss, had hated this enforced and, to him, hypocritical observance. In addition, he had disputed his parents' choices concerning his education and artistic career.

Clearly these were old, familiar grievances, but I have wondered if perhaps there was more to them than mismatched childhood recollections. For (apocryphally) Arthur had left Paris – where Richard was living, along with his wife – in the late 1930s to return to his parents, in Bavaria, after the news emerged that Mina was gravely ill with cancer.

Arthur was therefore in Germany for his mother's death in February 1937. And he was still there for Kristallnacht, in November 1938 – the pogrom against the Jews which brought beatings, arrests, murders, and the burning of synagogues and Jewish businesses. Arthur and Julius were both arrested and sent to Dachau concentration camp. Both men survived, to be released separately. My father, in his thirties, emerged physically and psychically damaged. As for Julius, the nice, mild-mannered man by then aged seventy-six, there is no knowing the effect of this experience on mind or body.

After that, the need to depart was incontrovertible and my father was permitted to emigrate from Germany in 1939, with a visa for Shanghai, but Julius's papers did not arrive as quickly and he could not accompany his son. My grandfather never left. He was deported to Theresienstadt ghetto/camp on his eightieth birthday, 10 June 1942, and died there the following February.

It's hard not to speculate on a more complex web of feelings that both distinguished and conjoined the brothers in the aftermath of these events. Did Richard feel any guilt, or jealousy, towards Arthur for his greater closeness to and involvement with their parents before their demises? Did Arthur? And what was the essence of their sibling relationship anyway? Were they friends, or merely relations?

At later moments, Richard would comment in correspondence that his brother was a good guy, a loyal companion through childhood. At others he expressed distaste at the thought of seeing him; they had nothing in common. But that was Richard: inconsistent even while engaged. Meanwhile, the bond of their family ties held, even if it never drew them close. As for Richard's sceptical, conflicted attitude to his German upbringing, it was fundamental to the artist he became. Perhaps this too contributed to the fraternal duality and the distance.

My uncle, seemingly, was ever the loner among the Lindners, his sense of his own creativity and identity setting him apart from an early age. In some families, an individual might take on the designation of 'black sheep' or 'plough' – cutting a lone furrow away from predictable terrain – and this role seems to have been his. The many interviews with and monographs about him reveal an intellectual, introspective man, with refined tastes and perceptions, and a large circle of friends, but touched with melancholy and always separate.

His letters reveal more – a kind of impatience with company and a low threshold for boredom. For all his apparent social sophistication, Richard the private man was scathing and judgemental. He made nice with us in 1967, but I doubt there was much joy for him in a bourgeois family home busy with marriage rituals. Our household offered little of the cultural depth he craved or the peace he frequently sought as a refuge from individuals deemed inadequate.

Arthur, a 'big' personality (and an endomorph to Richard's ectomorph, though both men were short), had a similar strain of absolutism. Either he liked you or he didn't, nothing in between. He was blessed with practical skills and mechanical aptitude, and, despite suffering his own share of tragedy, was probably a happier, less restless soul. More of a conformist than his brother, he expressed creativity too – in pottery, woodcarving, copper beating. He also enjoyed culture, but of the popular, more middlebrow kind. He was a member of the *Reader's Digest* book club. For many years our record collection comprised three LPs – folk songs performed by the Russian army choir; *The Threepenny Opera*, sung in German by a cast including Lotte Lenya; and the soundtrack to *Carmen Jones*. Richard's tastes were demonstrably more elevated. Even if Richard and Arthur had been close when young, or had shared more in the family, no stories of childhood larks or intimacies exist.

Arthur, nevertheless, seems to be the model in a number of Richard's early paintings – the chubby *Wunderkind*, seen with a piece of machinery in two works, both titled *Boy with Machine*, from 1954 and 1955. The central figures in these pictures, especially the former, bear a striking likeness to my father. But my initial assumption that this might be an indication of fraternal warmth has been tempered by the knowledge that Lindner's 'repulsive vision of the dreaming boy' was likely underpinned by the views of German psychiatrist Hans Prinzhorn, and represented the artist's deep interest in the links between insanity and creativity.[3] Richard, says critic Dore Ashton, believed that the sources of art could be sensed in the works of psychotics and children. 'The turgid children in his paintings of the 1950s are,' she says, 'in their unhealthy tumescence, clearly abnormal, particularly the male children.'[4]

What kind of backhanded compliment could it have been to apply his brother's likeness to a painting – one that would become iconic – that discussed genius but through the lens of the grotesque, the flawed and the doomed?

I am left, then, to speculate on Richard and Arthur. Did one wound or reject the other, or was there simply too little overlap? There are no records. They lived for a while in proximity to each other in Paris in the mid 1930s, seemingly a formative time for Arthur since both his children have related names. My sister (who is five years older than me) was named Madeleine after the Parisian church L'église de la Madeleine, and I am named for Richard's first wife, Elsbeth, of whom Arthur was apparently very fond.

There's a third angle to the 1967 visit, which relates to that same *Sergeant Pepper* album cover that cemented Richard's wider fame while also yoking him permanently, despite his disavowal of it, to the Pop Art movement. His visit to England that year included not only the trip to Stoke-on-Trent but time in London with

Peter Blake and his then wife Jann Haworth – the artists and designers of the album cover.[5]

Blake and Haworth had met Paul McCartney through his friend, gallery director Robert Fraser. McCartney had developed an interest in painting and was starting to collect, and Fraser was advising him. Fraser, who represented Blake and Haworth, was also, it seems, an early adopter of Lindner's work and had held an exhibition of Lindner paintings at his Duke Street gallery, which Haworth saw. 'I remember this being one of the first exhibitions at the Fraser Gallery. It must have been '62 because it was before I knew Peter,' she told me.

Haworth had already come across Lindner via a French magazine called *Aujourd'hui*, in which she had seen a photo of his studio, the shelves crammed with 'all manner of toys and collectable popular culture items'. Having found this article myself, I can see why it would have grabbed her imagination, stuffed as it is with images from *l'atelier de l'artiste*. Shelves overflow with wooden masks, dolls and coloured mechanical toys made of tin – walking miniatures, birds, a man on a bicycle. On another surface there's a collection of objects: a hair ornament from a nineteenth-century Chinese dancer; a photo of Richard's lost sister Lizzy; a leather doll found in the street; a mirror purchased at a Puerto Rican market in New York; an Indian doll; a postcard illustrating a French chateau, sent by the American artist Bill Copley. In an age of collage and colourful assembly, bric-a-brac and memorabilia, which the Blakes celebrated and turned iconic when it came to *Sergeant Pepper*, the appeal of this early magpie collection must have been irresistible.

Paul McCartney had had an idea for the album cover that involved the Beatles appearing in a British park, being given a formal presentation behind a huge floral clock and watched by an imaginary crowd. According to the Beatles' record producer George Martin's account, George, Paul and John (but not Ringo) gave Blake a list of the characters they wanted in this audience, but Jann Haworth, Robert Fraser and Blake himself drew up their own lists too. 'Peter Blake's list included Dion, of Dion and the Belmonts, Leo Gorcey and Huntz Hall of the Bowery Boys, Richard Lindner and Richard Merkin, both painters.'[6]

However, 'I can tell you,' Haworth says,

> the choice of Richard's appearance on the cover is mine. Peter now claims authorship of 100% of the cover (as does Paul McCartney, recently) but when I met Peter in 1963 he was unaware of Richard's work... So, to clarify, the Beatles chose just over a third of the heads that appear on the cover. Peter and I knew that wasn't enough to make a crowd. The idea had been that it was to be a crowd of their heroes – so Peter and I made the remainder of the choices and Richard was among those selections, along with Richard Merkin, Simon Rodia [a sculptor], Larry Bell [artist and sculptor], H. C. Westermann [satirical artist] and Mae West.[7]

(Haworth adds that 'of the few women that appear on the cover, none were chosen by the Beatles'. George Martin adds that if he had been asked for his heroes, he would have included R. J. Mitchell, the Spitfire designer from Stoke-on-Trent.)

The Blakes' first face-to-face meeting with Lindner had been in New York in November 1963, under the shadow of John F. Kennedy's assassination. It had also been a personally fraught time for the couple. Haworth had suffered a miscarriage before starting the journey, which obliged them to postpone their encounter with Lindner, originally planned for the beginning of their trip, to its final days. In Los Angeles the Blakes had been robbed twice. Yet their eventual visit to Richard's apartment is remembered fondly. Haworth saw for herself the toys and memorabilia that the artist was amassing. 'As you entered his apartment, by the door, there was one of those wooden "black-amoor" figures, with a tray – part of the collection.'

The three of them went out to dinner. 'We had a lovely meal, in a German or Polish area of the city. It was the capstone to my interest in Richard's work. He was hospitable and sweet.'

Then, in 1967, when Richard came to the UK and visited my family, the couple met him again.

After Christmas, Richard Lindner came back to London and we had many pleasant evenings together. Each evening he came in a different dapper outfit. He's as precise in dress as in mind. As always he was full of interesting comments. His reason for coming, he said bemusedly, was the Beatles cover. His nieces (English) were working out the people on the cover and got a few and asked their father about some of the faces that looked more antique and he named a few. 'And this one?' they asked, and he replied, 'Oh, that's your uncle.'[8]

This account by Jann Haworth strikes me in several ways. First of all, I envy her the intimacy she shared with Richard. Her comments on his style, her quotes illustrating his insights and wit embody the relationship I wish I had been able to enjoy with him myself. My uncle and I shared a passion for the arts. His was creative and groundbreaking, mine (a life in book publishing) more quotidian. Yet I sense – or fantasize – a connection or a dialogue we might have shared that was not available to me with the rest of my family. This ghost relationship has haunted me for years. Might I have found a 'fit' with him? Even more wildly, might he have done so with me?

But secondly, her description of him talking about my sister and me is wholly false. Or else it isn't my truth. Even if events had unfurled as Richard recounted them, did he think his nieces – aged sixteen and twenty-one – wouldn't have been able to pick his face out of a line-up that ranged from Elvis Presley to Mahatma Gandhi? More importantly, I remember very clearly the morning I opened my parents' newspaper, the true-blue conservative *Daily Express*, to find an announcement of the Beatles' new album, along with a full-page illustration of the *Sergeant Pepper* cover and a key to its characters. It was I who spotted Richard and pointed it out to my father – who responded, extraordinarily and exceptionally, by buying the album. Now we had four LPs.

There was no cosy scene of infant nieces with heads together poring over the album, nor was my father someone likely to identify the other faces. Richard remembered differently, or made it up. Did a homely family image that included his fame but differed so greatly from his own lifestyle appeal in some way? Was it patronizing? Or did he simply misremember?

Clearly he had a different view of Lindner-ness, and stood by that. A letter to me from late 1969 includes the afterthought, 'Unfortunately your parents, I believe, have a hard time to understand me and my life. But I cannot change my Personality [*sic*].' Arthur and Else had been included in the same arms-length bracket of bourgeois norms as his own parents. While there's undoubtedly an element of truth in Richard's assumptions, there's also some suggestion of vanity or pride or defiance there too, all perhaps aspects of the private man which exist alongside the many accounts of his warmth, gentleness and amiability.

After 1967, the brothers never met again, although the Christmas parcels kept coming, as did an intermittent correspondence from Richard in the form of postcards from New York, an eclectic, possibly emblematic visual record of Manhattan across the decades that includes Chinatown ('a touch of the Orient', 1963), the UN and the Unisphere at the 1964 World's Fair ('It dramatizes the interrelation of the peoples of the world and their yearning for "Peace through Understanding"').

As the years pass, the cards revisit various topics: money; a hope to visit (endlessly postponed); efforts to find enough time to paint. They express thanks for gifts received: a lovely pullover in 1959; another nice pullover in 1963. So the gift exchange was perhaps a two-way street, though the more imaginative direction seems to have been west to east.

One postcard from the 1960s – signed, oddly, as were several, 'Onkel Richard' though addressed to my father – was apparently written from a restaurant table in New York's German quarter. According to this missive, Richard was painting a lot, and had teaching obligations too – which paid well. But a visit that year was therefore out of the question. Piquantly, the message ends with a description of him in this restaurant, only ten blocks from his home. 'Everything is German here. Sausage and cakes cooked in the German manner. Definitely, during the war, they were all Nazis.' This was exactly what my father – who shared Richard's appetite for the food of their childhood alongside a blanket loathing of all living and dead German things – would have said.

More unusually, when my father was taken seriously ill in 1974, Richard sent a letter to his hospital bed. It opens, *'Mein Lieber Adda'* – a nickname for Arthur – drawn in green ink within a pink heart. The letter goes on to explain why Richard will not be coming to his brother's bedside during this year, which happened to be one of the crowning moments of his career, with an exhibition in Paris that travelled on to Rotterdam, Dusseldorf, Zurich and Vienna.

If only he had known a week earlier, Richard writes, but 'I'm just back from the opening of my exhibition in Vienna', and teaching obligations do not permit. Complaints about the miseries of travel in Europe follow, plus news of a new apartment purchased in central Paris. But then comes the insistence that Arthur spend recuperative time in Switzerland or Austria. Richard offers financial help. 'I know you and Else would do the same for me.'

It closes with hopes that Arthur will be *'schnell wieder* alright' (swiftly all right again). Such Anglo-German crossovers were familiar to me. My parents, when conversing with other German speakers, would switch back and forth without pause.

And then, finally, 'You were always the strongest one in the family... We are two old stubborn Jews. But I love you very much.'

And there you have it, a fragment of the diaspora translated into the parallel experiences of a pair of European brothers, their trajectories warped by malign history. One stays faithful to his belief in family and recreates a model of solidity in alien terrain. (My father's heavy accent and foreign features never allowed him to 'pass', yet his good-burgher status in Stoke-on-Trent led to degrees of acceptance by both business and social communities. And he struggled to achieve a degree of 'fit', if not for himself, then for his children. Jewish we might be, yet my sister was baptized into the Church of England and I into the Methodist faith. Camouflage was desirable, if not wholly achievable. And strange lines were drawn. When, for example, I wanted to go to the confirmation class that my friends were attending, I was not permitted. Evidently a prayer too far.)

The other brother embodies the triumph of art over circumstance. Richard's difference seems inherent. His impulses to reject his family and make his own choices of people and direction, begun early, were consistent and insistent. He found different families – creative and political people – in Paris and New York. He wove out of all this a body of art that allowed him to scrutinize and distance himself from glorious, atrocious European complexity. Even as his work evolved to embrace US commentary and iconography, he never forsook his continental origins.

Indeed, neither brother did, sharing instead an ambiguous allegiance to mainland Europe. While revolted by their experiences in Germany and France, they returned repeatedly to these countries and others within the continent, from the 1950s on.

With notable symmetry, my father died in Bavaria in 1989, in the country he despised beyond words, but after a meal full of nostalgic savour. Undoubtedly he assumed all the Germans in the restaurant were Nazis too. Richard found fame, a second wife and a lifestyle split between France and the United States. For each, Europe was both their undoing and their essence.

2

Germany 1901–33

JULIUS (also called Jüdell) Lindner was born in Altona, the westernmost urban borough of the German city state of Hamburg, on 10 June 1862. At that time, Altona, perched on cliffs above the River Elbe, was still administered by the Danish monarchy, serving as Denmark's only real harbour with direct access to the North Sea. It passed to Prussia in 1866, and was incorporated into Hamburg in 1937.

Julius was the younger of two sons born to Louis Lindner, a furrier and cap maker, and his wife Hannchen Salomon. Louis died in 1884 and is buried in Hamburg's Jewish cemetery; Hannchen died in 1911. Julius's brother, Salli or Sally, four years older and born on 4 March 1858, became a musician and artist, and married Anna Heim, a Catholic woman from Bavaria. Perhaps Sally and Anna are the couple Richard is said to have admired. 'Among the members of his family he remembers most fondly [are] an uncle and an aunt who were variety artists. The uncle, Lindner recalls with pride, wrote popular songs that were heard throughout the street in Bavaria.'[1]

Described as a businessman by the Nazis, and a travelling salesman by my father, Julius married Mina Bornstein in Hamburg on 11 January 1893. She was seven years his junior.

Mina's parents, Louis Bornstein and Henriette Reichenbach, were German Jews living in Williamsburg, New York, for reasons not discovered. One of seven Bornstein siblings, Mina had been born in the United States – a fact which, forty years later, suggested an escape route when the Lindner menfolk were trying to flee Nazi Europe. Her date of birth was 25 July 1869. She returned to Germany in 1889, at the age of twenty, and the couple were married four years later. A first child, Lizzy (aka Lizzie or Lissy), was born a year after the wedding, in 1894.

The seven-year gap that opens up before the Lindners' second child, Richard, came along, on 11 November 1901, is explained by a recent discovery – records of two children who did not survive: Arnold, born in 1895, who lived for one month; and Curt, born in 1896, who died at just over six months.

Then, according to the Centre for Bavarian History, 'Around half a year after Richard was born, the family moved to Christiania, today's Oslo. A second son, Arthur, was born to the Lindner family in 1904, and an address book makes it clear that in 1905 the Lindners were living in Nuremberg.'[2]

Thus Hamburg's small but essential role in the story draws to a close, but, before we depart from the city, two items, symmetrical in shape, are worth recording. Julius's last known address, before he was deported to the concentration camp where he died, was in Munich, a city that has not permitted the installation of very many of the tribute stones to persecuted and murdered Jews called *Stolpersteine*. This is due to the efforts of a woman named Charlotte Knobloch, referred to by the BBC as a Bavarian Jewish leader, who considers the stones – which are in fact small, square, discreet metal plaques – offensive, even though over 70,000 of them now exist, in more than 1,000 European cities, the work and commemorative offering of a tireless man, Gunter Demnig.[3]

Mainly, the *Stolpersteine* (literally, 'stumbling stones') have been set in the ground at the place of the last known, freely chosen dwelling of the Jew whose life they record. But in Munich, because of the ban, the few stones that have been laid are to be found in the walls of buildings owned by sympathetic supporters of the project. For this reason, there is currently no stone in Munich for Julius Lindner.

But there is one, it turns out, in Hamburg, at Schulterblatt 64 in St Pauli, a district which belongs to Hamburg-Mitte now but for a while was part of Altona. According to Peter Hess, who was central in arranging for the *Stolperstein*'s installation, Richard Lindner was born at this address.

The other item, also square in shape, I found in my parents' cuttings album devoted to Richard. Much of this material, ageing under cellophane sheets, was supplied by the artist himself, in whatever spirit of inclusion or affirmation. Amongst the news of TV shows and gallery openings, there is a yellowing square of German newsprint dated May 1971, headed 'Lindner Schau in Hamburg'. The article announces an exhibition including Richard's work at a Hamburg gallery. With an amusing period flourish, it concludes, 'Our picture shows Esther Daniels from the pop group Black Pearls in front of the Hamburg Lindner poster.' An attractive black woman in a busily patterned blouse smiles over her shoulder, turning her face from an image packed with Lindner iconography – a female with those lips and breasts parked in the centre of what might be a Wurlitzer jukebox or a pinball machine.

It's hard not to speculate on Richard's emotions at this exhibition, and press coverage, in the early 1970s. Although he had taught briefly at Hamburg's Akademie für Bildende Künste in 1965, he was now seeing proper, high-profile professional recognition in his birth city, in the nation that had worked so thoroughly to expunge him. Local boy finally made good.

For his father, the trajectory was downwards, into cruelty and suffering. Now, at least, with the *Stolperstein*, it is concluded with a gesture of valuable if inadequate restitution, arranged by strangers.

(In a final, debatable gesture, a matching *Stolperstein* has been placed next to Julius's, commemorating Richard Lindner himself, even though he survived Nazi oppression.)

The Centre for Bavarian History's page goes on to recount that the Lindners moved home multiple times in Nuremberg in the early years of the twentieth century. Another source (the *Catalogue Raisonné*[4]) lists some seven different addresses in the city; yet another says ten. This multiplicity, according to the centre, confirms that the family's circumstances were modest. However, Arthur never described his upbringing as materially deprived. He did remember learning to ride a tricycle down the long corridors of one of the family's Nuremberg apartments. And Richard asserted that one of the figures in his landmark painting *The Meeting* was modelled on the family cook. So not perhaps such an impoverished or cramped home.

My father also recalled that Julius was often away for his work. In an apocryphal story, he remembered his father travelling as far as Russia in the pre-revolutionary era, returning home with shocking stories of poverty, of children with no shoes. Whether Julius's income was adequate or not remains obscure, but we do know that while the boys were still young, Mina began a home-based business, making corsets.

My father's memories of this activity were dim and somewhat dismissive. He described the domestic workplace as a *Kaffeeklatsch* (gossip shop). But, for Richard, the corsetry manufacture would come to carry a larger, more complex and ineradicable significance. As a creative artist, his work is littered, from beginning to end, with corseted women: women in armour, women with breasts pushed up and exposed, women laced up tight.

This fact alone has resulted in many pages of analysis and critical comment. Brian O'Doherty, for example, in a *New York Times* review of Richard's exhibition at Cordier & Ekstrom in 1964, described the women as 'clumsy Valkyries stuffed like heifers into the elasticized trapping of female hardware. The underwear is dissected with a fixation that becomes symbolism in art and in life a form of fetishism.'[5]

Writer Hilton Kramer, in an obituary for Richard, called the iconic figure 'the corseted temptress', representing the fatal woman seen in much of Lindner's work.[6]

Curator Judith Zilczer identified Lindner's vision of the corset as 'a complex and multivalent symbol'.[7] It would be one of several in his lexicon, a repertory of symbolic characters and shorthand motifs that would characterize his painting 'voice'.

At that time – the early 1950s – when Richard began to include corsetry in his art, the garment itself was being pensioned off as standard female underwear, giving way to brassieres and 'roll-ons' or foundation garments and garter belts, part of the youth revolution and the shift away from restriction and rules. Feminism would push the boning and lacing further into the dustbin of history, or even, as with bra-burning, set fire to it.

Incorporating such items in a work of art was thus in part a deliberate gesture towards bygone eras, as well as an invocation of bourgeois sexual thrills. By including one loaded image, the artist might shock those whose prudery and smugness he was happy to deride, while invoking temporal distance. He was also encasing his women figures in mysterious armour, lending strength while suggesting an idealized, impregnable form.

Were Lindner's women victims or warriors? Multiple quotes by him suggest he saw them as the dominant, certainly the more fascinating gender, riddled with secrets. In his pictures the strappy underwear could imply violence and sadomasochism, often complemented by other items that hook, bind, trap, confine, victimize, dominate – masks, boots, dark glasses. Questions of power and control become inescapable, as do torture and public eroticism, aspects of Lindner's open-ended dialogue between his European past and his New World future.

Meanwhile, Lindner's attitude to women – those close to him and those observed later, on his research strolls through the streets and shopping emporia of New York – would be a recurrent, obsessive facet of his work and personal life.

Jann Haworth's Pop Art riposte to the whole corsetry issue was to make several three-dimensional artworks – soft sculptures – out of the corseted females in Lindner's paintings. 'I've done several homage pieces about his work,' she told me,

> The Lindner Doll (2 versions) and The Lindner Dolly with Steinberg Clothes, and a small version of The Lindner Doll. We met for the last time in '73 when I had my show at the Sidney Janis Gallery. I have a photo of Richard and Sidney in front of The Lindner Dolly with Steinberg Clothes.[8]

The Lindner Doll (1963–4), fabricated out of silk stockings and vinyl, is three feet high and dressed in a multicoloured corset that leaves the blonde woman's breasts exposed. It has an oddly innocent aspect. The work was shown at the Fraser Gallery and sold to the Belgian surrealist E. L. T. Mesens.

A Lindner Dolly with Steinberg Clothes (1967) can be seen at the Museu Coleção Berardo in Lisbon. This one is naked, apart from elaborate hat and boots, but comes with a wardrobe – including a corset, of course – to be attached at will. It is subtitled 'A Homage' [sic]. I asked Haworth if Richard liked the dolls. She said he did.

Equally influential on the young Lindner's imagination was the city of Nuremberg itself, notable especially for its genius artist son Albrecht Dürer and cobbler-poet Hans Sachs. It is a quintessentially German city, walled, dense and narrow, characterized by medieval quarters, some of which were painstakingly rebuilt after their destruction in World War II. Its principal tourist attractions include a famous item of torture, the Iron Maiden – a kind of mechanical spiked coffin which skewered its unhappy victim as it slowly closed.

The town was famous too for its production of toys, and Lindner would become a lifelong collector of them – mechanical figures made of tin, dolls, clowns, monkeys, Napoleon, Uncle Sam, Mickey Mouse. Friends would give them to him. He enjoyed the bright colours and would come to include elements of play in his art.

Nowadays, Nuremberg's place in history is dominated by its links with Hitler, both pre-World War II – notably the rallies – and afterwards as the location for the trials of Nazi war criminals. It's a Bavarian stronghold, famed for its beer halls, sausages and gingerbread. Lindner held a deep ambivalence towards it. In 1977 he discussed his roots there with Stephen Prokopoff, Director of the Museum of Contemporary Art Chicago, remarking that as a child he sensed the cruelty of the city, because of its history of torture and its medieval mentality, aspects that drew Hitler to deem it the capital of the Nazi Party. According to Dore Ashton, he felt 'he was reared in the wrong town'.[9] John Russell, in his obituary, quotes Richard as telling him, 'I did drop in on *The Meistersingers of Nuremberg* once, but I couldn't sit it out.'[10]

The family household, as recalled by my father, was *bürgerlich*, meaning – to him – middle class, solid. The one family group photo that exists is of a large gathering, seated around a table set with coffee, sparkling wine and a heap of fruit on a glass platter. The room is large, with tall windows, and has a distinct Beaux Arts flavour. An intricate metal and glass chandelier hangs over the table. On the back wall, an art nouveau wall ornament is surrounded by small, framed pieces of art. The decor and homely table linen suggest a comfortable domestic scene, not an impoverished one, but perhaps the gathering was not held in the Lindner household.

My father sits at front left of the photo, grinning like the *Wunderkind*, in a suit and open-necked shirt. He is perhaps six or seven. Richard sits behind him, giggling, with eyes closed. In embarrassment or pleasure? This is the only picture of him with a full head of hair. It is also a rare picture of the brothers together.

Next to Richard sits their mother Mina, looking the camera straight in the eye, her expression quizzical. Then comes Julius, his head partly obscured by his wife's up-do, but he is smiling above his winged collar. At the back of the table sit an elderly, formal, slightly dazed couple: my great-grandparents, on Mina's side, both of whom died before World War I. The camera flash freezes the group at what looks like a happy moment, history far in the future, though not far enough.

I believe Mina's sister, my great-aunt Else, is included among the other nameless figures on the right, a dark-haired, self-possessed young woman in a pale blouse with dark trim. She is the large-bosomed aunt who features alongside Richard, in a sailor suit, in *The Meeting*.

I met *Tante* Else once, in 1958, the first year my parents could afford to take the whole family on holiday. Choosing to slake my father's yearning for European mountains and lakes, they had reserved rooms in a hotel in Switzerland, the Hotel du Lac in Spitz, on Lake Thun. Brochure pictures showed a see-saw sitting in the hotel's waters. I, at seven, was thrilled about this more than anything else.

To reach Thun, we had to take a ferry across the Channel, then drive through Europe, a journey that required significant planning. Bespoke maps were ordered from the AA, beds were constructed for my sister and me across the back seat of our car – the plan was to drive through the first night – and the portable spirit stove (found in a post-war US Army surplus dump) was packed, allowing us to cook a bacon-and-eggs breakfast atop the white cliffs of Dover before boarding ship. This twenty-five-mile sea trip would expose the fact that my sister suffered from seasickness as well as carsickness.

My mother was an appalling map reader as well as an impossibly anxious passenger, facts which put additional pressure on my father, who, heroically or perhaps foolishly, was doing all the driving – four days non-stop in each direction. The stress would also bring on one of his mammoth headaches. These and a peculiar wound on his leg were the physical legacy of his imprisonment by the Nazis.

My mother's other job, when not misdirecting our choice of road, was to wield Arthur's cine-camera and obey his instructions about what and when to film. Thus miles of motorway driving were captured, with a particular focus on car crashes. I, however, in the back seat, was more magnetized by bullet-pocked buildings, the number of men who lacked limbs and the fact that many of the people, in various countries, looked like us.

Our route was planned around visits to those outlying family members who had survived the conflagration of World War II. My sister and I had not been abroad before, nor met any of these relatives. The strange, intense, near-hysterical encounters that took place discomfited us. There was one small branch of the family tree in Brussels. From there we travelled to Aachen, on the German−Dutch−Belgian border, where my mother had spent her entire pre-war life surrounded by a large extended family, all murdered in the Holocaust. We were welcomed at a flat owned by Uncle Moritz and his wife Maria. It smelled peculiar. But Moritz − a relative by marriage − was kind, giving us gifts of clothes and chocolate.

From there we headed south, to Munich, a journey that could not be completed in a single day. Overnight stops were selected randomly, wherever a hotel could be found. At such places, or in restaurants and shops in Germany, my parents would be complimented on their faultless German. When asked if they were natives, they would deny any such thing. They had learned the language at school, they would claim. The country was not theirs.

In Munich, we would encounter the last round of relatives − a pair of Bornstein aunts. The first, Matilda, was curly-haired, roly-poly and smiling. Although also related by marriage, she seemed to be a virtual mirror image of Arthur's assertively large, upbeat Bavarian character. We would meet her again on future visits.

From Matilda, we moved on to an assignation in the gardens of the Nymphenburg Palace, later the setting for Alain Resnais's classic film *Last Year in Marienbad* (1961). Here a woman dressed all in black awaited us. This was *Tante* Else. My sole memory − and my sister's too − is of her tears. Nothing else, just a woman who clutched my father − 'Arthur, Arthur' − and wept with the intensity of a funeral mourner. Smiling Matilda and weeping Else, the matched faces of the dramatic muses of comedy and tragedy.

★

Not much is known about the Lindner children's education, but music seems to have featured prominently. One source (Alexandre Alexandre) has Richard telling a friend that he had not done well at school, and had therefore been apprenticed by his father to a hardware store. 'This was not at all to Richard's liking.'[11] So he took up music in rebellion against his parents and became a pianist. His brother Arthur remembered Richard as a talented musician. Dore Ashton corroborates this. She says Richard studied at the Nuremberg Conservatory, 'preparing for his brief career as a concert pianist (he gave only two public recitals) when Germany was defeated'.[12] She also reports that as an art student he often earned a little money by playing piano accompaniment in the movie houses.

The publication *Commercial Art and Industry* presciently devoted multiple pages in its May 1934 issue to an article by Amos Stote called 'Meet Richard Lindner'. This chirpy piece recounts that Richard

> had musical hands, or at any rate his parents thought so. Wishing to make young Richard very happy, as well as themselves, papa and mama Lindner decided the child should perform on the piano.
>
> Being, temporarily, a dutiful child, Richard Lindner became a pianist. In course of time he became a very good one. So good that he actually gave concerts and, more surprising still, people paid to come and hear him.[13]

Richard's own assessment? In an 'About the Artist' appendix to *The Continental Tales of Henry Wadsworth Longfellow*, which he illustrated in 1948, he commented, with understated acid: 'I spent years at the conservatory, studying music. I became a pianist, gave two fairly successful public concerts, and was pleased with neither my profession nor myself.'[14]

There is less dispute over reports that his older sister Lizzy was a gifted singer. Richard saw her perform in *La Traviata* in 1913. My father's apocrypha include casual mention of notables like Feodor Chaliapin, the world-famous Russian operatic bass, dropping in for tea. Lizzy died in 1915, at the age of twenty-one, of influenza − or meningitis, as my father had it, caught while singing to the German troops.

Either way, her death apparently devastated Richard. Of all the Lindner family members, she would seem to have been the one for whom his feelings were uncomplicatedly positive. Her picture would be affixed to his noticeboard in New York, and she is included in his autobiographical painting *The Meeting*, young, fleshy, sexualized (à la Balthus), running her fingers through her hair, one leg provocatively bent at the knee. A couple of family photographs of her depict a rather more innocent figure: sweet-faced as a pre-teen in one, plump and Teutonic, dressed in a dirndl, in another. No records of her life, career or death have been traced.

Whether having trained as a hardware-store salesman or as a pianist or both, in 1922 Richard enrolled, aged twenty-one, at the *Kunstgewerbeschule* (applied-arts college) in Nuremberg. The reason?

> One day, in the street, I met a former classmate whom I had not seen for years. He promptly asked what I was doing, and I replied I was discontented, that I was playing the piano. He said he was a painter (and looked it), attending an art school where there were some very beautiful girls. He was happy, he said, and looked it. I ought to come and paint too, he said; it wasn't hard at all. I took his advice, accompanied him to the art school, and became a painter. I never played the piano again.[15]

At the college, for two years he studied life drawing, oil painting and commercial art, sometimes under Max Körner, a painter who was also director of the masterclass for applied graphics at the Nuremberg school. But even here, according to one of Richard's closest friends, Alexandre Alexandre, there were signs of pulling away, since, being both gifted and independent-minded, the young artist did not rely on his teachers' guidance.

Evidently Richard was taking his first practical steps on the road to self-expression and self-knowledge. Later in life, when sharing some of the wisdom he had gleaned about creativity with his lover Evelyn Hofer – who was twenty years younger and trying to forge her own artistic career as a photographer – he insisted, repeatedly, on the unique spark of creativity that springs from the individual and the work. No matter the métier, it was that single, personal connection which, at its most honest, would give rise to art. Experience was everything.

Meanwhile, the switch to art was a second major rupture. Breaking away from a life in music that was making him unhappy, choosing instead a seemingly carefree, bohemian life in art must have been a welcome contrast with the suffocation and discord Richard experienced at home. But there must also have been a sense of fit. Like his friend, Richard must surely have discovered that art wasn't hard at all – because he was exceptionally good at it.

Had this never suggested itself before? And how did his parents feel about yet another, probably not inexpensive change of direction by their questing oldest child? Perhaps, in a household stricken by the loss of three out of five children, an element of tolerance or indulgence – or even resignation – became woven in.

Lindner was a success at the college, winning prizes for advertising design in a toy competition, and other contests – for the A. W. Faber Company, the Albati cigarette factory and the Haeberlein-Metzger *Lebkuchen* (gingerbread) bakery. This last resulted in 'no money, but a whole basket of *Lebkuchen*'.[16] He was also nominated as a 'master pupil'. Then, in 1925, he moved to Munich, where a friend was studying at the academy.

> This friend asked me to visit him at the academy, and when I entered the beautiful old building I was transported. I walked through many hallways and galleries and when I reached his studio I saw two or three artists sitting there painting and smoking and talking. In the center of the room stood a fat naked woman who was posing. The atmosphere was so congenial... It was like a dream world![17]

This quote, taken from an interview shortly before Richard's death, seems to fold the Nuremberg and Munich study periods into one, or perhaps glides over the earlier period spent at an applied-arts college. It continues:

> I gave up music and applied for entrance at the academy. I was accepted and stayed there for three years. I became a master student. I learned all the basics and my first works were very academic still lifes. I learned how to draw extremely well from very bad painters. I soon found out that from a good painter you never learn anything. Picasso and Matisse were terrible teachers. The only thing a good painter can do is stimulate you.

(In later years, for financial reasons, Richard would become a teacher of art himself, at the Pratt Institute in Brooklyn, New York.)

Another move, this time to Berlin, came in 1927. A file in art agent Betty Parsons's papers includes an autobiographical note written by Richard stating he attended the Academy of Berlin in 1928, to study painting. The irrepressible Stote has it that the move to Berlin resulted from a letter to a celebrated theatrical producer in the capital, who invited Richard to create stage decor and costumes.

He liked Lindner's work for the young artist was already giving evidence of his remarkable ability to depict the amusing and the grotesque... He not only cartooned people but he cartooned and caricatured things, habits, human emotions, city scenes and buildings. Whatever he drew, it always seemed to come out with its weaknesses and peculiarities. Made laughable.[18]

Talented though he was, Richard's income at the time was patchy and meals were not always reliably available. Stote recounts Richard's ownership, at this time, of a large white angora cat whose need to eat apparently took precedence over its owner's. But then Lindner had a passion for cats, a lifelong love affair.

Hungry or not, Richard was thrilled with capital-city life:

I lived there for two years – 1927 and 1928. Well, Berlin was a fantastic city. I mean, it was criminal! It was rotten with talent! *Everything* was going on. It was as George Grosz had depicted it, full of decadence and meanness. It was lurid and perverted and marvelous. And so was Paris, when I finally got there. Paris was also rotten, but with big, big talent everywhere.[19]

In 1929 or '30, he moved back to Bavaria, this time to Munich. He had been offered a job as graphic artist – or art director? – by Knorr & Hirth, a publishing consortium producing both books and newspapers, including Munich's *Illustrierte Presse*.

My crumbling artefacts include a copy of this paper dated 15 February 1931. My uncle's contributions can be seen on various pages, including a cartoon of Neptune, complete with tattoo and admiring fish (with striking lips). Richard appears in photographs too. The back page shows him lolling on a sofa with a woman, underneath a full-wall cartoon of what is probably his work. The drawing includes lecherous men and saucy women with naked breasts, linking the Lindner iconography familiar from his American work to its European origins.

Other family photos, dated 1932, show him clowning around in a studio, half his face concealed behind a gargantuan fake moustache. Best of all, perhaps, is the publicity or advertising shot confected as an April Fool's joke for the Munich newspaper. In a postcard-size photograph, Richard can be seen holding an issue, its date of 1 April prominently visible. He is dressed in drag, a bit like Old Mother Riley (a British music-hall act featuring a man in a bonnet and dress). His centre-parted wig features a complicated topknot. His frock has embroidered cuffs and puffed sleeves. There is a pince-nez on his nose. His expression is amused. He seems to be a happy man.

And why not? Richard was, by various accounts, a political animal and surely aware of Germany's disturbing national shifts, yet his own arc was rising. His job was prestigious and seemingly pleasurable. Better still, he had a wife. He had married Elsbeth Schülein, a fellow student in Nuremberg, on 24 June 1930, and the couple had settled in Schwabing, in northern Munich. Elsbeth continued her studies at the Meisterschule für Mode (the fashion-design college), or possibly taught there, as one photograph suggests.

Naturally, I have taken a great interest in my namesake, yet I know very little about Elsbeth, and the few facts that the family possessed since my childhood or earlier have been worn smooth by repetition.

However, recent research has turned up her immigration file at the US National Archives, and this at least has clarified some simple facts. She was born on 1 September 1906, in Nuremberg. Her father, Benno Schülein, was born in Ellingen, Germany, in 1876, and died in 1928. Her mother, Johanna, was born in Munich in 1879, although by the time of Elsbeth's arrival in New York she had moved to Buenos Aires and applied for citizenship there.

Elsbeth had two sisters, Lotte and Paula, who preceded her to the United States and would assist her in making the same transition. Lotte settled in San Francisco and Paula in Chicago. Later they are credited with supporting Richard and Elsbeth when they arrived in New York in the early 1940s.

The archive forms describe Elsbeth in 1941 as five foot six, weighing 120 pounds, with brown hair and grey eyes. The accompanying photos show an exhausted woman whose smile does not reach her eyes. Yet what is indubitable about my aunt is that, with her flawless skin, dark eyes and hair, and widow's peak, she was a beauty. A clutch of earlier photographs exist, some with Richard, some of her at work. In one, Richard gazes possessively at her, clutching her arm, crowding her space, while she gazes away, modestly, a small smile on her lips. The one showing her teaching at the Munich school sets her against an audience of female students, attentive in white overalls as she gracefully arranges fabric on a form.

In yet another, undated photo, the couple are working together at a tiny folding table. Both clutch pencils. Elsbeth wears spectacles. Her specialism was fashion and clothing, a fact that seems to be reflected in her own tasteful dress.

Little of her work can be found today, although the New School in New York possesses seven original drawings for adverts she created in the 1940s for Saks department store, donated by Juke Goodman, the store's art director, and his wife in 1982. They are pen-and-ink drawings of jewellery, gloves and hair ornaments, created with exquisite precision. Brooches, necklaces, earrings, cuffs; made of stones, marcasite, linked loops of precious metal – all are rendered as precisely as if machine-made, yet their backgrounds suggest something else, a more European, fanciful and curved line that echoes Richard's book illustrations.

★

Historically, what happens next shifts my relatives' story more directly into the public sphere, as the achievement and pleasure of Richard's early married life are interrupted by massive catastrophe. With Adolf Hitler's ascension to the role of German Chancellor in January 1933, many Germans – socialists, Jews, intellectuals – heard an alarm sounding. Richard and Elsbeth were among them, and decided to leave.

For Richard's brother, Arthur, however, it seems the danger was less apparent. If I know only scraps about my uncle's existence in pre-war Germany, I know even less about my father's. His youth, education and professional life are largely blanks. I believe, though, that he grew up to enjoy a fulfilled early life, working as a dentist in a rural location in southern Germany, near a lake. He loved to ski in winter – bare-chested, he would relate with typical machismo, because the sun was so intense. He had a passion for cars and can be seen smiling in photos, perched on the running boards of vehicles he pretended to own but which, in fact, were far beyond his means. During this phase, there seems to have been little or no overlap between Richard and Arthur's social circles.

Arthur too, however, was married – and divorced – before the war, facts I only learned in the late 1960s. These revelations came one sunny afternoon, in the garden of our home in Stoke-on-Trent. I, who thought I knew this man, was predictably shocked to learn of an entire previous chapter, one that could have eclipsed the family of which I was a part. I know nothing about this first wife in pre-war Germany, only that she was not Jewish and that the marriage was childless. If not, Arthur told me, he would never have left her.

3

France 1933–41

THE move away from a birth nation, the decision to emigrate, brings about a kind of molecular disintegration. The culture of origin, once set aside, can never be resumed as before. The émigré has joined a floating population, at home everywhere and nowhere.

As Richard himself put it, 'I feel I might be American, German, Indian... The feeling of really belonging does not exist anymore. I don't believe in nationalities anymore.'[1]

My parents' decision to establish themselves in England and in Stoke-on-Trent gave me a nationality and a home town, and yet these have felt largely arbitrary, something I might easily shrug off. Even as a child I felt distinctly separate from my peers, who had history in our neighbourhood, and generations behind them. I have never claimed to be English and was aware from those early days how much I *didn't* know about that identity. The unknowing only intensified, a deficiency that would never be remedied.

After university in Birmingham, I moved to London and created a career and my own identity there. It was skin-deep, but it was the best I was going to get, and it served for some thirty years. It is in London that I have come closest to feeling a sense of belonging, even though I haven't lived there for most of the last two decades. Leaving London to live in the United States, even though this was freely chosen, was therefore a testing business. Richard said, 'When I arrived I was afraid of not knowing anything and having to start all over again.'[2] My own fears were both identical and borne out. I felt as abandoned and invisible in America, at the beginning, as I feared I would. Some years of depression followed. However, my struggles and complaints seemed ridiculous, offensively trivial even, compared to those of my parents, and Richard and Elsbeth. Perhaps that knowledge also contributed to my difficulties.

For the Lindner brothers, and my mother too, emigration was a matter of life and death. Theirs was the tunnel focus of desperation. Did they dare to look back, or forward, to an imagined return? Etched for ever on my mother's memory was her last pre-war conversation in Germany, which took place on the platform at Aachen railway station as she waited for her train to Holland and then England, in August 1939. She was leaving behind her mother and two sisters, all of whom would be murdered. But before she could depart, clutching her small suitcase and the few Reichsmarks permitted to an emigrating Jew, she was approached by an SS officer. His advice/command: 'Never come back.'

In the light of this, it's difficult not to forgive the separation anxiety with which she blanketed her children, even though understanding didn't make it any more tolerable.

For my father, the encouragement to reconsider his view of home was couched in yet harsher terms. His papers, lodged at the Imperial War Museum in London after his and my mother's deaths, include a pass issued by Esterwegen concentration camp, in the Emsland, stating that he was imprisoned there from 10 March to 2 August 1935. So he had been a prisoner of the Reich years before Kristallnacht.

The Emslandlager (Emsland camps) were a series of fifteen Nazi labour, punishment and prisoner-of-war camps active from 1933 to 1945 in a marshy district of Lower Saxony.

According to the subsection of the JewishGen website on 'forgotten camps', little is known about Esterwegen. Indeed, the local administration denied its existence. JewishGen describes it as 'a *Strafgefangenenlager* – "punishment camp for prisoners". Of course, the living conditions in this camp were the same as in the concentration camps: tortures, executions, forced work in the swamps until death, etc.'[3] Another site – Gedenkstätte Esterwegen (The Memorial of Esterwegen) – reports that 'from 1934 to 1936, Heinrich Himmler, Reichsführer SS, was directly responsible for the concentration camp'.[4]

Concentration or punishment camp – either way, why was my father there and how did he come to be released? Any certitude, at this juncture, seems unlikely to be found; of course, he never spoke about this episode. It's possible, however, that his marriage to an Aryan woman became the cause of his suffering. Once in power, the Nazis had moved with lightning speed to strip the Jews of rights and freedoms, starting in April 1933 with attempts to force them out of the economy. Jewish businesses were to be boycotted, and not just shops and traders, but doctors, dentists (like Arthur), lawyers, and so many more. Jews with jobs in the civil service were forced to quit them.

By September 1934, it was possible to declare formally that Jews were henceforth second-class citizens, with fewer rights than Aryans. At this juncture, sexual intercourse or intermarriage between Jews and Aryans was forbidden. There was huge pressure on such 'mixed-race' couples to separate. I will never know if my father's marriage was already faltering, or whether the decision to end it was a question of politics and survival.

More to the point, in the rancid climate of Germany in the mid 1930s, a person of independent mind and *Untermensch* status might easily fall foul of the authorities. The Nazis were busily transferring people who came to their attention – Jews and non-Jews, communists, socialists and liberals alike – into the camps to 're-educate' and make good, quiescent Germans out of them. It was an effective method of reducing vocal and practical opposition, and my father clearly learned his own lessons there.

It seems likely he left the country soon after his release, in the late summer of 1935. His reasons for choosing Barcelona as his new home are unknown. But he didn't deny that he spent some time there, and his printed name on the backs of photographs with Spanish content – notably bullfights – would tend to confirm it.

This brief professional life in photography took my father from Spain to Paris, but not beyond. What must it have been like, working in a visual medium alongside a brother whose whole life was art and who was struggling to find employment? Did picture-making in the French capital – the closest Richard and Arthur probably came to sibling rivalry – unite or divide them?

For Arthur, the move from Germany to Spain was but the first step on a path of swerves and recalibrated expectations. Next would come Paris, then Germany again, then England, then Australia. He thought Britain would only be a transitory phase, and Shanghai his destination. Later, he wanted to settle in Australia, but my mother refused to cross U-boat-threatened oceans. He would finally settle in the UK – and find some peace.

Similarly, if he had had career plans, these evolved constantly with forward motion. There would be no more dentistry: his German qualifications held no value in other countries. So, first came photography, later furniture restoration, odd-jobbing, some time as a dental technician, finally watchmaking and jewellery. He was flexible and enterprising. He morphed.

For Richard, the geographical interruption was different. He did not have to abandon his last. His work was his identity and his talent was portable. He was able to hold on to that sense of self, at least, through the coming vicissitudes.

Moreover, his background – and Elsbeth's – meant the possibility of connecting to an existing network in their new home city. And indeed, Paris did offer the Lindners a circle that would sustain them, both in and beyond France. Friends made there became part of the foundation of a new, enduring 'family' in America. They were the kind of friends who would help you find work, or assist in saving your life.

Was my uncle a political animal? There are a few signs of it – in an interview in 1973, when discussing life in pre-war Munich, he refers to 'our force, the Social Democratic Party' as if he had been a member.[5]

He also had recollections of seeing Hitler, often, at the Café Heck, where Richard and his friends from *Simplicissimus* (a German satirical magazine) had a regular table, as did Hitler with his supporters Georg Strasser and Hermann Goering. Richard's dismissal of the future Führer is couched in characteristically negative terms – his laughable taste in clothes, his bourgeois aspirations, his inadequate artistic gifts:

> He dressed in black, with a black artist's hat, black suit, black tie; he often wore high boots, riding boots and carried a whip... He was always careful to make a good impression, to appear as a good bourgeois among the people of this café... and he always wanted to be with artists.[6]

Apparently Hitler knew Richard was an artist – 'At the time I was very well known in Munich.'[7] – and would always show a kind of aspirational respect towards the group, despite the insults the artists heaped on him.

These comments don't answer the question of why Richard felt the need to leave Germany immediately Hitler took office. His explanation, in this same interview, is not especially clear, although he mentions friends who became Nazis, tapped phones, and the knowledge that his name was 'on the list'.

I spent no more than a single day in Germany after the Nazis took over... I was going to the movies twice a day, and one day I came out of the theatre and Hitler was in power. It was in the afternoon, around two o'clock... That evening there was a great torchlight parade. I couldn't go back to my house because I knew they were already there to arrest me. It wasn't a question of my Jewishness but of my politics. I turned around and around. I had to join my wife one way or another... So I jumped into a taxi... The torchlight parade was a surprise to the inhabitants of Munich: it was improvised. My taxi entered the parade – to the right and to the left there were SA carrying torches. I was seated there in the taxi, holding my nose because of my profile... We moved very slowly. Sometimes we had to wait. My fear grew.[8]

This dramatic, indeed cinematic account ends with Richard slipping away from the flickering light and crowds, to be joined by Elsbeth a few days later. 'That, if you like, was my worst experience with the Nazis.'[9]

As fellow artist Larry Rivers put it: 'In 1933, the day after the Nazis took over and Munich's number one failed artist became Chancellor, Richard became Jewish and immediately left for Paris. Until that day Richard hadn't paid much attention to the Jewish part of his German identity.'[10]

And so to Paris, where, in the early 1930s, the immediate associations are with hedonism and modernism, American exiles – Gertrude Stein, Ernest Hemingway – flooding in, African American jazz arriving in the form of Duke Ellington and Fats Waller, to meet the African art of Picasso.

In fact, much of this cultural ferment took place in the preceding decade – *les années folles*, the madcap years – but the mood lingered and is reflected in the surviving Parisian photographs taken by my father and developed at his studio at 8 square Léon-Guillot, in the fifteenth arrondissement, on the Left Bank. These black-and-whites, dating presumably from the later 1930s, include girls kicking their legs among a froth of petticoats at the Folies Bergère and a zinc bar complete with massive coffee-making equipment and a blinking tabby cat. There's even an image of Arthur himself – taken by whom? – standing in a narrow alley, chatting, one knee bent as he props himself up with a foot against the wall. The shadows around him are deep and long.

Dore Ashton's account of the city in this era conforms to cliché too – artists and writers living in ancient hotels, eating cheaply and spending whole days in cafes. Montparnasse is regarded as the centre of Parisian pleasures and literary politics.

But other accounts evoke a city which, beyond its intellectual and artistic elite, was being infected with fear and partisanship. Exiles had already arrived in significant numbers, from Africa, Italy and Eastern Europe, during the 1920s. After Hitler's ascent to power in 1933, more than 20,000 Germans arrived during the remainder of the year, and by the end of the decade over 55,000 émigrés from Germany had passed through France.[11]

The diary of a German aristocrat, Count Harry Kessler, himself a refugee on account of his socialist sympathies, expresses upper-class Aryan outrage at the descent of Germany into pariah status. In 1933 he wrote that 'the abominable Jewish boycott has begun... a criminal piece of lunacy... This is the most horrible suicide a great nation has ever committed... Clearly sadism, a hysterical pleasure at [the] flow of blood and suffering, plays an important part [in the Nazi mentality].' Kessler concluded that it amounted to 'a pathological feeling of power in the imposition of torture... suddenly active among hundreds of thousands'.[12]

Kessler fled to Paris too, where he observed the flood arriving in 1933:

'Some by first-class coach with steamer trunks, others by the skin of their teeth having lost nearly everything.' They included bankers, publishers, journalists, writers, philosophers, pacifists, politicians (Socialists, Communists, and liberals), and especially Jews. Even the most eminent nonpolitical figures were in danger simply by being Jewish: under threats of violence the famed conductor Bruno Walter was shut out from conducting in Leipzig, Frankfurt, and Berlin, while no less a personage than Albert Einstein lost his position at the Berlin Academy of Sciences. 'Lack of intellectuality is the most terrible thing about the Hitler regime,' Kessler noted that October. 'For the time being, though, there is nothing to be done about it other than creating a haven where the intellectuals can take refuge.'[13]

Anti-Semitism was no stranger to the French capital or to national culture either. The Dreyfus affair had taken place fewer than four decades earlier. More recently, an outbreak of cholera in the 1920s coincided with an influx of Jews to Paris, giving rise to knee-jerk accusations that Jews were vermin, to accompany the stock references to blood-sucking capitalists.

To be fair, though, as Andrew Hussey, author of *Paris: The Secret History*, points out, 'Hatred of foreigners was a common and usually admirable virtue and Jews were not at first especially hated more than any of the other races who had found their way to Paris.'[14]

But the post-Hitler influx intensified fears, and February 1934 saw riots on the streets of the capital. Now positions on the left and right only hardened, first as the socialist Front Populaire took power in 1936 and later as the Spanish Civil War and then Hitler's military preparations entrenched opinion.

It was against this background that Richard and Elsbeth established themselves, in 1933, within a community of German and central-European refugees – creative people, writers and intellectuals – that included journalist Joseph Bornstein, photographic agent Maria Eisner, who would later be central to the formation of the Magnum photography co-operative, architect Paul Lester Wiener and writer Hans Possendorf.

Richard had apparently visited the city before, in 1930, and perhaps already knew its neighbourhoods. Or possibly the couple's finances might have defined their choices. Either way, the Lindners found accommodation on the Left Bank – first in rue Jules Chaplain, in the sixth arrondissement, later in the thirteenth's rue de la Glacière – and began to look for work. Although in his biographical statement at the Parsons Gallery, written in 1954, Richard says he was 'painting and illustrating for magazines and books' during the years 1933–9, other reports suggest that commissions were scarce.[15]

He had time on his hands, and, according to his close friend Alexandre Alexandre, could be seen 'walking through the rue de la Glacière in Paris with his shopping bag, to buy meat, vegetables and cheese for his lunch, as was his habit'. Or else he might lie 'lazily on a couch in his atelier in the Hotel des Terrasses, reading one of Strindberg's novels, which he admired'.[16]

Alexandre's comments come from a 1948 essay called 'The Poster as a Work of Art', a dissertation on the advertising posters that Richard painted for the Barnes piano factory in 1936 – joyous, comic watercolours, evoking a Victorian Europe of musical entertainments and group gaiety – which Alexandre reports were causing a sensation in London. He argues that these ads, these works of art, spring from the combination of Lindner's genius – 'His work... stands out through its originality, its flashes of wit, and its artistic conception: it reveals the future master' – and the influence of Paris. The city's effect was 'confusion, rapture, intoxication'. And what artist, Alexandre declares, is not transfigured by the city's enchantment?[17]

He describes Richard experiencing the École de Paris's met-
amorphosis like a rebirth: 'He suffers. Like a child, he starts
learning to walk all over again.' The underemployed artist is
depicted exploring ideas, wandering the city, absorbing exhibitions at the Louvre and elsewhere. He is mocked by his friends
for reading and looking more than working. But Alexandre
defends him: 'They are wrong. To master the Paris experience
is a gargantuan task for a true artist.'[18]

And Richard, many years later, still remembered something
similar:

> Like most of us who left the country, we were more or less
> in a kind of a cloud. We had left our country and we had
> never been outside of or without a country, so the whole
> thing was a little bit confusing. And we were young too. And
> before I could develop as an artist, really, as a mature artist,
> I was leaving my country and I was in France and I had to
> start all over again in some way or other.[19]

Evenings might be spent at the Dôme, the artists' cafe in
Montparnasse, where 'he is an amusing companion, brilliant.
But his jokes and anecdotes are filled with gentle self-irony. All
the grandeur he sees in the arts in Paris make him feel small.'[20]

For Elsbeth, the same struggle did not, apparently, hold true.
The intensifying political atmosphere had not yet disrupted
Paris's role as fashion capital of the world and those French
magazines devoted to women's clothes – notably *Vogue* and
Le Jardin des Modes – continued to publish, preoccupied as ever
with couture and beauty. In January 1939 *Le Jardin des Modes* was
advising its reader to dress their hair in a low chignon '*à la duch-
esse de Windsor*', and even as war approached it was encouraging
followers to keep up their standards: 'For those who are at the
front, you must stay how they would like to see you. Not ugly.'[21]

Elsbeth's illustrations appealed to both publications and the income from their commissions is said to have supported both her and her husband.

Lucien Vogel, the general manager of *Le Jardin des Modes*, later moved to New York and became one of Elsbeth's sponsors in her 1941 application for US citizenship. His letter of support, while no doubt over-egging the pudding, nevertheless spoke warmly of 'her peculiar talent and her very specialized knowledge of the reproduction of printed fabrics'.

In this same period, Richard and Elsbeth's base in Paris would serve as a beacon of rescue for Arthur and his father, during their efforts to find a lifeline out of Germany. Although Arthur had joined the couple in Paris at some point in late 1935 or 1936, he left them, as mentioned, in 1937 to return to his parents and was arrested on Kristallnacht, 9–10 November 1938, to be imprisoned with his father in Dachau. Julius, arrested on 10 November, was released on the 15th. Arthur, however, was still in the camp in December 1938; in a letter to Julius on 18 December, written from Block 10, he asks if his father has heard anything from Richard about their emigration. He's hoping to be back home with Julius this week; meanwhile, what about the passes? Did he have photographs? Escape to France was evidently his intended plan for both of them.

And in a Red Cross letter from Julius to Arthur – by now deported to Australia by the British – in April 1941, the father asks about letters from Richard and Elsbeth. 'Hopefully I can soon be with them.' He says he has received affidavits for January 1942 from Leopold (perhaps the mystery uncle referred to by Richard who had worked at Macy's in New York for fifty years[22]), after which he will soon be there.

Julius didn't know that the couple had already left France, and that by 1942 he would be deported to Theresienstadt.

★

In his *New York Times* obituary of Lindner, dated 18 April 1978, John Russell commented, 'In Paris, he lived, like many other refugees, from hand to mouth. If he could work against the Nazis, he did. If he could make some money as a graphic artist, he did. If he could meet with French artists, he did. And he painted on his own account.'

Richard's own description was comparable to Alexandre's:

> I went into exile in Paris, and soon felt at home in this true native city of twentieth-century painting. Daily I saw the pictures which in Germany had struck me as revolutionary; daily I saw their painters and was amazed to find that here, ten years later, they were already classics... In Paris, too, I began to take a lively interest in the Surrealists. It was not so very far from Bosch to them.
>
> Paris has a hundred ways of enchanting a painter. I would come from the museums, stirred by the pictures of the great French painters, and walking down a street I would think I was seeing them everywhere. Motifs of Watteau and Delacroix and others down to Renoir were present and alive: there were the same lights, the same colors, figures, and faces. Perhaps this dual existence, this continuity and identity of art and nature, is the great secret of the French painting tradition.[23]

Lindner later claimed that he started to work as an artist proper in 1950, and didn't want to include his earlier graphic and commercial work in the *oeuvre*. Nevertheless he did paint during these pre-war years, even if not yet in oils. The work from pre-war Paris overlapped with his graphic-design commissions and the examples that survive – such as a drawing of his wife asleep, or the watercolour depicting the view from Maria Eisner's apartment in Paris – seem comparatively realistic and literal, also sometimes soft and romantic.

Although Richard demoted these early originals, he kept a collection of them, which meant that they were transported from Europe to the United States during or after the period of transition. No details are apparent as to how he did this, but the fact of it suggests they had significance to him, at least at the time.

The *Catalogue Raisonné* lists some twenty-nine works dated between the years 1933, when Richard and Elsbeth arrived in Paris, and 1939, when they were arrested. (There are a further twenty-four 'Early Works', according to the catalogue, the period of which ends in 1950.) Several are illustrated in the catalogue: portraits done in pencil, or ink and watercolour; landscapes of statues in city squares and vistas from windows. Several of them prefigure the leap Richard would later take to create his own unique pictorial language – a billiard table, a *Wunderkind*, a cat.

Alexandre describes other efforts:

He paints little. But he paints. He is especially inspired by the end of the last century and the beginning of this one – the scintillating, glittering decay... His pictures contain much humour, irony, even more satire and a hefty portion of deeper meaning...

One of his last Paris pictures, perhaps the last, *Spring 1939*, was painted in colours reminiscent of the washed-out tawdry colours of artificial wreaths. A young couple in love, shy, embarrassed, almost children, in the cafe La Closerie des Lilas. Through the window one sees houses illuminated by the eerie light of an approaching storm.[24]

What is described here sounds innocent, sentimental and obvious in comparison with the paintings that would emerge from Richard's return to the École de Paris in 1950. By then, realism, cliché, landscape and identifiable locations had disappeared, to be replaced by claustrophobic interiors and enigmatic characters, few of them appearing innocent.

Perhaps more important is Paris's recurrent role in Richard's life as cultural cornucopia, as world out of time, as the European match for his Manhattan other self. Its art absorbed him, and its literature too – he would later paint a pair of formative portraits of authors who had captured his imagination: Verlaine and Proust. In the last chapter of his life, it would be an alternate home, the place where he lived and worked six months of the year, while always returning to New York for inspiration and a jolt of adrenaline.

But now, in the late 1930s, despite the richness, camaraderie and sense of possibility, other emotions were coming to the fore. Fear, alienation and a growing awareness of personal peril pervaded daily life. With war imminent, restrictions began to be imposed on immigration numbers, and internment/detention camps were being created. After Britain and France declared war on Germany on 3 September 1939, the French government simultaneously ordered the rounding up of German and Austrian nationals – 'enemy aliens' – to be placed in these camps. Richard and Elsbeth were arrested and, separately, imprisoned.

4

Uprooted

THE crisis arrives. But who is best prepared for catastrophe? The 'strongest one in the family', Arthur? Richard, sensitive and sceptical? Enigmatic Elsbeth? My mother Else, whose character and choices in her home city of Aachen had been circumscribed by a domineering father? If you were worldly, or modest, or toughened, or sheltered, would any of these serve you better?

Speaking as a second-generationer, blessed with my own little suitcase of catastrophism, I can only dream – literally – of the eventual entry into that most feared present tense, barbaric racism right there in the same room. Perhaps consciousness refines down to a pinpoint. Perhaps a fog descends. Or is there 360-degree vision, the adrenaline supercharge that might propel one through nightmare? All of the above?

Richard's own account of his experience, softened by ten years and a layer of his sardonic wit, went as follows:

> I spent seven years in Paris, painting and loving the city more and more, reading Balzac and Stendhal and Flaubert, every day drinking cheap French wines, and sometimes the good ones. I even thought I loved the French – until one day in September 1939, in a curious confusion which I have yet to forgive them, they put me into a concentration camp because Hitler, that frustrated painter who was my enemy too, had gone to war against them.[1]

One version of the facts recounts that he was 'arrested when war was declared for being a German and "consorting with the enemy"'. He was imprisoned at the Palais des Sports and released five months later. He entered the French army and still later tried, but without success, to join the British army.[2]

'When France fell [in 1940], he was interned again, at Blois, before being singled out to guide the German troops invading the country. Fully aware of the new dangers before him, Lindner fled on foot across France, reached unoccupied territory and then Marseille.'[3] These biographical notes, compiled by one Maïten Bouisset, seem full of questionable remarks. I would particularly like to understand what 'singled out to guide the German troops' might mean.

The facts are more likely to be those recorded in Richard's immigration file, though even that has its discrepancies: 'Between September 1939 and April 1940 I was interned near Blois; upon my release I served with the British Expeditionary Force in France, until my demobilization in July 1940. From July 1940 until February 1941 I lived in Toulouse and Lyon.' His immigration visa application makes no mention of the BEF, specifying that he spent the months April to June with the French army in Le Mans.

The camp near Blois was Villemalard. The website Jewish Traces offered some background, now removed, to these French detention centres in which Richard and Elsbeth and so many others were confined.[4] It included the eyewitness statements of two men sent, in 1939, to visit the numerous French camps, which included Huriel, Domérat, Catus, Marmagne, Braconne, Ruchard, Saint-Just-en-Chaussée, Loriol, Limoges, Libourne, Battereaux Farm in Bengy-sur-Craon, Villemalard, Villerbon, Chambaran and the camp for women in Rieucros.

The first of these statements explains that 'alien gathering centres' would be used to house subjects aged between 17 and 65, Saarlanders, Germans and Austrians… Men between the ages of 18 and 48 can enter into the Foreign Legion for the duration of the war. In addition, the refugees who are entitled to asylum, that is to say, the Saarlanders, the former Austrians and those who have in their passport the words 'refugee from Germany', and are up to 55 years old [will be] taken as service providers: they must carry out work for the National Defense, and will be assimilated into the military.

This probably explains Richard's recruitment into the French army.

My father's apocrypha included a different story – one he simultaneously disparaged – of Richard, handcuffed to a chair while detained by the French, jumping out of a window as the Nazis came in through the door. Arthur tended to reserve the more emphatically masculine traits of the Lindner family for his own personality. He laid little store in the notion of Richard as an action hero or even a pressed soldier.

But, surprisingly, a more elaborate version of this same story came to light in my research for this book, in an interview with Richard's second wife, Denise, conducted shortly after his death. The artist Larry Rivers interviewed her, as part of *his* research for an obituary:

Denise tells me that when the war came [Richard] was put in a camp by the French as a German refugee. Some Parisian friends got him out. She continues: 'Then he joined the French army to fight the Germans. There he is, a German in a French uniform, and he is a Jew. He had to do something. So he *walked* to Marseille. You know how far it is from Paris? He had no money, nothing. On the way he met a young French girl, and he went to a hotel with her and spent the night there. In the morning the French police – the Gestapo – walked in.

They find out he is a German Jew and they handcuff him. He was lucky, they handcuff him to a chair instead of the bed. Then the girl went into the bathroom to get dressed; she was pretty and the policemen wanted to have a peek at her, so they both went in after her to see her getting dressed. Richard at this point jumps out the window still handcuffed to the chair and runs all over the city. In a cafe, a sympathetic group frees him from the handcuffs. He found some people he knew, and he joined the underground.'[5]

We come to a crossroads of choice here. Who is right? Arthur, the sceptical younger brother with more moxie? Richard, creative, romantic, not conventionally heroic, who might have enjoyed sketching this farcical scene from comic-opera old Europe, complete with libidinous officials, saucy wench and derring-do? Or Denise, whose own relationship with a husband forty years her senior adds another filtering layer over reputation and memory? While fighting the urge to be loyal to my father, I have to allow that the tale may have a kernel of truth.

Comedy aside, whichever version of the above holds the most water, it is beyond dispute that Richard and his fellow 'enemy aliens' were suffering nightmares of privation and danger as they were tossed back and forth by the convulsions of France. The country had imprisoned them after declaring war against Germany in September 1939, only to release them into a larger national flood of refugees the following year, after its military defeat.

Now the victorious German troops occupied the northern three-fifths of France, including Paris and the entire Atlantic seaboard, while Vichy France – deemed a shorthand for collaboration and capitulation – controlled, nominally at least, the southern remainder. Hence the possibility of an escape route out of the Mediterranean ports.

Hungarian Jewish writer Arthur Koestler, best known for his anti-Soviet novel *Darkness at Noon*, was another victim of these events, arrested in Paris in October 1939 and taken to the Roland Garros tennis stadium,

> which had been converted into a makeshift processing centre for 'undesirable aliens'. After nine days of sleeping on a tennis court strewn with straw and huddling under the bleachers, Koestler joined five hundred other prisoners at Le Vernet, an internment camp located southwest of Toulouse…
>
> Koestler lived a grim existence at Le Vernet, his days organized around twice-daily roll calls and manual labor. He was assigned latrine duty, carting foul-smelling waste bins over icy terrain down to the River Ariège. Care packages from friends supplemented the camp's meagre daily rations of eleven ounces of bread and watery beef broth.[6]

The men's heads were shaved. The camp was surrounded by barbed wire.

Richard's experience, I assume, was a variation on this theme.

With the fall of France in 1940, 'Lindner and thousands of other refugees were released from concentration camps only to face anew the dangers of arrest either by the German occupation forces or the newly formed Vichy government in unoccupied France.'[7]

In his own words, 'When Hitler's armies overran France and the country fell apart and half the people covered the roads in flight, my personal flight took me amidst the deluge and I saw the horrors and metamorphoses of modern war and was shaken, as a man and as an artist.'[8]

By early 1941 he had reached Lyons, where, with the aid of Elsbeth and their friend Maria Eisner, he was able to obtain papers and sea passage for New York. Before leaving, he wrote to a relative, Amy Amschwand. (Amy, the sister of roly-poly *Tante* Mathilde whom I met in Munich in 1958, lived in Switzerland and could act as communication point for the scattered family members.)

Richard's letter, dated 13 February 1941, reads:

Dear Frau Amschwand

This evening I am leaving for New York… My wife has already been there for 14 days. We were separate for a year. For the last 7 months my wife was in Casablanca and I in Lyons. We have not exactly spent a pleasant time since the outbreak of the war. I was in French concentration camps, likewise my wife, although not as long as I. My ship… leaves Lisbon on March 14. Through friends and relatives, my wife made this trip possible for us. I have heard no more from Julius nor from my brother… My address in … New York, Elsbeth Lindner, 504 West 112th Street, New York City.

Yours, Richard Lindner.[9]

Elsewhere, my father, finally freed from Dachau on 25 February 1939, was being swept along on a different tide. His papers at the Imperial War Museum include documents from the Jewish Benevolent Society dated 28 July of that year, which trace Arthur's route out of Germany – supposedly with a final destination of Shanghai – to England, via Belgium, on a three-day transport: Cologne, Aachen, Ostend, Dover, Deal and Sandwich, concluding at the transit camp in Richborough, Kent, on 31 July.

This camp, also known as the Kitchener Camp, was an ex-army training barracks taken over by the Council for German Jewry in an effort to support refugees. 'In August 1939, the camp housed almost 3,000 Jewish refugees from Germany, all between eighteen and forty-five years old, many of them skilled or professional men and almost all hoping to emigrate to the United States or elsewhere.'[10]

No formal confirmation exists of Arthur's visa for Shanghai – it belongs among the apocrypha. (Some years later, my family would become acquainted with a couple who did find refuge in Shanghai's wartime Jewish ghetto. At the end of the conflict, heading back to Europe, they had converted their remaining wealth into sewing-machine needles, which had been immensely valuable as currency in the Far East. Arriving in England, they discovered that they were paupers.)

Even if my father did possess a transit visa, it would appear to have been overtaken by events. After Germany invaded Poland and war was declared, Arthur's onward plans were eclipsed and it seems that he stayed in the Kitchener Camp at Richborough until early January 1940.

Unbeknownst to Arthur and his fellow inmates, a debate was being conducted, at government level, about the future of the camp's inhabitants – a somewhat gentler, more British version of that same debate that had taken place in Europe, but one that arrived at its own kinds of brutalities.

With the nation now at war and borders closed, what was to be done about the male enemy aliens of military age already in the country? Should they be interned en masse? Partly because of the shortage of available premises, and the cost, this option was – for the moment – voted down. Instead, it was decided that tribunals should be set up across Britain, to consider all male enemy aliens over sixteen and decide whether restrictions should be imposed on them.

The job of these tribunals was to sort the refugee individuals into one of three categories: A for those to be interned, B for those not to be interned but still subject to restrictions, and C for those who could remain at liberty.

Arthur naturally fell into the group 'subject to oppression by the Nazi regime upon racial, religious or political grounds... They will be hostile to the Nazi regime and ready to assist this country rather than assist the enemy.'[11] Such individuals were to be placed in category C. This is confirmed on Arthur's 'Male Enemy Alien – Exemption from Internment – Refugee Form', dated 18 October 1940.

He had also worked hard at the Kitchener Camp, and been noticed, as was reflected in an affidavit, dated 5 January 1940, stating that Arthur Lindner had been there since 1 August 1939,

> and has during his stay been in charge of our workshop for arts and crafts. In addition to all kinds of repairs which he carries out most skilfully, he has won our admiration for his exceptionally artistic design and craftsmanship. We feel sure that his high qualities of character and comradeship will make him an asset to any community he will settle in, and our best wishes accompany him for his future.

With this glowing end-of-term report, Arthur seems to have been sent on his way. His route (for reasons I don't know) led him away from Kent, on the south coast, in early 1940, towards the Midlands, where he would meet my mother.

Else Levy had had no intention of settling in Stoke-on-Trent when she arrived in England in August 1939. Her own plans had been to wait in London for her mother and her unmarried sister, and then travel as a group via Liverpool to America. But war began, her family never arrived, and she was left, an unworldly twenty-four-year-old, to fend for herself. Exempted from internment and apparently in need of sponsorship, she was taken in by a kindly blue-collar family named the Longhursts, who had stepped forward on her account.

Thus she ended up in gritty, industrial Stoke-on-Trent, a city of coal mines and bottle kilns (used in the pottery industry), living in a *Coronation Street*-style terraced house. Mr Longhurst, a bill poster, would arrive home at the end of each working day filthy from the glue he had used to paste advertising sheets to large hoardings. He would bathe in a tin bath in front of the fire.

This sight, and the locked food cupboard at the private home where Else found work as a (hungry) domestic servant, ranked among her most prominent memories of the time.

Nevertheless, Arthur and Else managed to find each other in Stoke, two souls who, despite a twelve-year age difference, shared sufficient culture and optimism to think they might have a future. And they did, after one more brutal episode.

The early months of World War II – September 1939 to April 1940 – became known as the 'Phoney War', owing to the relatively low level of activity on the Western Front. But when the Germans began to sweep through Western Europe, vanquishing Belgium, France and Holland in May and June, Britain's own fear of invasion now came to the fore, along with suspicions of a fifth column – of secret spies, possibly with foreign ancestry – covertly aiding the German troops.

The subject of the internment of 'enemy aliens', whether enemies or not, resurfaced and more restrictions were imposed on the refugee community. In May 1940 it was decided that category-B refugees were to be arrested, both men and women. Then, later in the month, permission was granted to the chief constables (heads of British local police forces) to arrest category-C individuals 'where there are grounds for doubting the reliability of an individual'.

As individuals go, my father was about as reliable as they come. Nevertheless, he was arrested yet again, on account – as family mythology would have it – of violating the blackout. Was he foolish enough to have allowed a chink of light to show, to catch the eye of a passing German bomber? If he did, it must surely have been by accident. But no matter. Arthur was arrested, on 3 July 1940, and sent to join the interned masses now being prepared for deportation.

This, incidentally, was a not-undistinguished group, including as it did Dr Martin Freud, son of Sigmund; John Heartfield, artist and acclaimed anti-Nazi; Richard Friedenthal, novelist; Kurt Jooss, Germany's leading choreographer; Otto Neurath, renowned Austrian statistician; Kurt Schwitters, celebrated artist; and so many more.

But little of that mattered. Fully focused on defending its own shores from possible invasion, Britain did not want to devote the resources necessary to keeping thousands of Germans and Italians – of whatever value – behind bars, or barbed wire, on UK soil, and had already petitioned Canada to take some of these people off its hands. A batch of some 2,500 Germans and 1,500 Italians were the first to go, shipped off to Canada in June on the passenger liner the *Duchess of York*.

Appeals were made to other nations – Australia, South Africa. Meanwhile, another vessel was being prepared for departure, the *Arandora Star*. She sailed for Canada from Liverpool on 1 July, carrying some 1,600 men including crew and guards. That same night, off the coast of Scotland, the *Arandora Star* was torpedoed by a German U-boat and roughly half of the lives on board were lost.

While this tragedy briefly cast a cloud over the treatment of the refugees, deportation plans continued. Moreover, Australia had come forward and agreed to absorb 6,000 internees. So another vessel was readied, the *Dunera*, a troopship designed to hold 1,500 passengers. She would set out on a two-month voyage to Australia, packed with 3,000 internees. My father would be one of them.

It would be fair to say that not all of the men who sailed on the *Dunera* went unwillingly. Some had been told they would be released when they arrived in Australia; others were happy enough to leave Britain, fearing the Nazis would soon invade. I'm not sure Arthur, with his new commitment to Else, fell into either group. Undoubtedly all were nervous that their ship might meet the same fate as the *Arandora Star*.

And rightly so. The *Dunera* sailed from Liverpool on 11 July.

Early the following morning, and despite efforts to disguise her route, she was spotted by a U-boat in the Outer Hebrides and two torpedoes were fired at her. They scraped her hull but did not sink her.

One major disaster had been avoided, but something else was already at play with the men on board. According to my father, the *Dunera* crew were not regular sailors. Britain's war effort had absorbed all the merchant seamen who would normally have served as crew. Instead, the vessel was manned, he said, by criminals, released in exchange for their contribution to protecting the nation. Other accounts suggest that the guards were soldiers who had been evacuated from Dunkirk, embittered and bearing grievances. Whoever they were, this group was put in charge of a large contingent of men who had, in many cases, already suffered immense loss and trauma. Some of the passengers were survivors of the *Arandora Star*. Their treatment during an eight-week journey aboard a 'hell ship' would became a national scandal.

According to an article in the *Jewish Standard*, the men were told

> they could each carry eighty pounds of luggage, would be given satisfactory accommodation, and would be treated like ordinary passengers aboard ship. But within a few hours they were to find that they were in the hands of a savage, murderous and villainous band of soldiers who treated them worse than any Nazi prisoner had ever been treated in a prison camp.[12]

This may have been an overstatement. Nazi camps were worse than the *Dunera* scandal, although both experiences were abysmal.

First of all, the men and their luggage were searched on the docks at Liverpool and systematically robbed.

Valuables were stuffed into sacks or disappeared openly into
the pockets of the searching soldiers... Appeals to the officers
standing by were fruitless. Attempts of protest were quickly
suppressed... All these searches were carried out without any
discrimination, accompanied by acts of violence, and resulted
in the loss of an enormous amount of money, valuable articles, toilet necessities and important documents which have
never been recovered.[13]

Next the men encountered their accommodation, below decks,
which was so overcrowded that they slept on tables or the floor
during the whole voyage. The hatches were kept battened down,
the painted-over portholes kept closed. The men were lit by
artificial light and breathed air that entered via ventilators. The
upper parts of the ship – and the fresh air – were out of bounds,
sealed off by barbed wire and sentries with bayonets.

The lavatories – approximately twenty-four seats for 1,600
men – were horrible, and the decks were often awash with
vomit, urine and excrement. Diarrhoea spread through the ship.
Shaving was forbidden for the first five weeks; soap and towels
were rationed; an epidemic of skin diseases erupted.

There was one exercise period on deck of fifteen to twenty
minutes each day, with internees of all ages walking or running on instructions, often accompanied by a string of oaths
and sometimes by blows from rifle-butts as well.[14]

The food was monotonous, often inedible. It consisted of
smoked fish, sausages, potatoes, rancid butter or margarine,
and maggoty bread. One *Dunera* captive remembered 'sitting
on the floor with a mug of soup, carefully removing the bodies
of little white maggots before I drank it'.[15]

And the thieving continued, often at night, as troops with
bayonets came through the cabins, taking watches and wedding

rings, slashing the lining of clothes in search of valuables. Even the officers were criminals. One, who was asked to take two canvas bags of valuables for safekeeping, never returned the goods.

There were beatings and insults, threats and stabbings. Mental torture and abuse were applied daily to men already debating whether life was worth living. And reports suggest that the small number of actual enemy aliens – Germans with Nazi ties – were treated better than the larger population of refugees.

Was this treatment as savage as existence in Esterwegen or Dachau had been for my father? No. But it was mean and rough, predatory and punitive. It expressed rapacious opportunism in the face of suffering.

Needless to say, Arthur never shared the details of his time on the *Dunera*. He viewed much of his wartime experience with shame. To be a prisoner wounded his sense of masculinity and self-determination. His mantra was 'Kick or be kicked'. The Jews had been kicked. He had never elected to be a part of their group, anyway. He was Jewish by birth but his family was non-observant and as an adult he claimed to be an atheist.

Instead, what he did say about the voyage to Australia was that he learned rudimentary English onboard, by reading and then rereading a Mickey Spillane novel. And it's true that his English was never very good.

As I type, I have at my elbow two items that survived the whole horrible experience. First, there's Arthur's suitcase, made of chestnut-brown crocodile skin. It's a small piece of luggage with leather straps inside and metal studs at the corners. It looks as if it belongs amongst those heaps of ransacked suitcases discovered at Auschwitz and Belsen. It pleases me to think that it accompanied him from Europe to the Antipodes and back, as a tangible reminder of a civilized era presently lost, perhaps to be regained.

I know he had the case on the return voyage, since there's an ancient label pasted to it, coloured red, blue and white, announcing the Blue Star Line of the Australian and New Zealand Service. In the centre is his name, and underneath, on the line for Steamer, he wrote: '*Stirling Castle*. From: Sydney. To: Liverpool.' The cabin number is illegible.

The other item is a small wooden box, handmade, hinged in brass and with a sprung metal tab to keep it closed. Inside, carved into the lid, is a pictorial of the voyage out. The five continents, islands of polished wood, are visible, set in a choppily gouged ocean. A dark line runs from the British Isles, top left, round to Africa and then on to Australia. Tiny nails, mere pinheads, have been tapped into the land masses to indicate where the *Dunera* stopped. Freetown in Sierra Leone, then Takoradi, Ghana. Then Cape Town, and finally Australia – first Fremantle, then Sydney.

He made the box himself, carved the trip into it, with who knows what tools.

The *Dunera* docked in Sydney on 6 September 1940, and 'a mountain of damaged and unmarked baggage was dumped on the Sydney quay'.[16] Soon after, the passengers, whose physical condition had shocked the Australians, were moved by train – a thirty-hour journey – to a railway terminus called Hay in New South Wales, where a camp awaited them.

> The camp was built around a former air-strip, with a double barbed-wire fence, four watchtowers armed with machine-guns, and thirty-two wooden barrack huts set in a fan formation. Within days, Hay's fearsome reputation was borne out. The temperature soared to over 100 degrees Fahrenheit and the notorious 'Bricklayer' wind began to blow with gathering strength.[17]

This would be home for thirteen months.

The men lived twenty-eight to a hut, sleeping in double rows of bunks, one above, one below. Mosquito netting was deemed a fire hazard, so hessian was used in the air vents instead, with questionable success. Yet, according to historical record, the internees made fewer complaints than expected, and those they did make were largely against the British who had so abused them on the journey.

Their status was confusing. Neither free men nor criminals, they were living behind barbed wire in extreme isolation. The situation was Kafkaesque, compounded by an appalling climate. 'Hell and Hay are the hottest places in the world,' the Australians would say. Correspondence was permitted, but only two letters home per week, each with a mere twenty-two lines per letter, and these were heavily censored. Surviving letters unsurprisingly reflect the internees' unhappiness at being cut off from their families and their European origins, as well as their strong anti-Nazi opinions.

Yet, despite all its discomforts and hardships, Hay has a

distinguished reputation in the annals of prisoner history. One inmate called it 'a small working republic'.[18]

The internees were not defeated soldiers but a cross section of working folk, many of them intellectuals, and they were equipped with a remarkably diverse range of skills. Partly in order to exert a measure of control over their circumstances, partly to right a tilted world, partly to distract themselves, they organized the camp into four departments: Administration; Culture; Hygiene and Maintenance; and Catering. Subcommittees were devoted to education, recreation, medical and dental treatment, and so on.

As well as moulding their difficult circumstances into an orderly, gratifying daily regime, the men made it their business to create a formal record of events on the *Dunera* – the '*Dunera* Statement' – which attracted attention first from local officials and eventually from the British government. But additionally, as my father's papers bear out, the inmates pooled their talents. Furniture was made from local wood, and sandals from old tyres. There was a vegetarian restaurant. Lectures were given, on topics such as atomic research and Shakespeare; there were musical recitals performed on home-made instruments, and theatrical performances, including of *The Good Soldier Švejk* and *Journey's End*.

Arthur returned from Hay with multiple drawings of the place, done by him and his fellow prisoners, as well as a volume of verse from assorted hands, and examples of the paper money that was printed and used. (He had also managed, according to the 'Internee Report' filed in the Australian National Archives, dated September 1940, to hold on to his steel wristwatch and gold wedding ring. How he hid them from the tirelessly marauding sailors is a mystery, although he later said that he spent hours on the *Dunera* dismantling and reassembling his watch, just for something to do. Perhaps it was in bits when the thieves came along. The existence of the wedding ring is even odder, given his unmarried state at the time.)

In a letter to Else from Hay, dated December 1940, Arthur refers to the 'regrettable mistakes' made with regard to the internees – this was Churchill's phrase, apparently – and the extreme temperatures. He closes with 100,000 kisses.

In truth, he always claimed to have enjoyed Australia. He liked the people. If Else had agreed to join him, he would have stayed, and I would have grown up yearning for distant English culture, like Germaine Greer and Clive James did.

But he was released in October 1941, after a British official arrived at the camp to arrange compensation for the men's losses and also to determine who would be allowed to return. Repatriation was offered early to men who signed up to serve in the Royal Pioneer Corps, and it seems that Arthur agreed to join this non-combatant unit even though there is no record of him actually serving in the ranks. However, a small, handwritten card found in the Isle of Man Enemy Aliens archive records his arrival in the UK 'ex-Australia'.

His pragmatic choice had granted him a passage home as one of a group of 338 internees on board the *Stirling Castle*, a voyage that that would come as a marked improvement over the outbound trip. This ship was transporting troops (Australian, presumably) blessed with a splendid intolerance for anything substandard. Arthur would happily recount the reception of a meal (of liver) which was deemed subpar and which the soldiers slung – plates, meat, cutlery, the lot – out of the portholes.

Back in the UK, internees were now being released again, some 1,000 per month during late 1940 and early 1941, and so when Arthur arrived in early 1942 (according to an 'Aliens War Service' pass) he was allowed to stay at liberty. And according to marriage records for the borough of Paddington, London, the wedding took place there of Arthur Lindner and Else Levy on 17 September 1942. He had survived, to be rewarded with a new wife and an opportunity to start (yet) again.

In 1942, Arthur wrote to Frau Amschwand in Zurich, as Richard had done from Lyons in 1941. Clearly some correspondence predated Arthur's letter, because he makes relieved reference to 'news from James and Mathilde'.

But he also observes, 'We are all depressed about Richard and Elsbeth. Sadly, there is nothing we can do.'

5

Elsbeth

A WOMAN named Elsbeth Lindner arrived in New York on 29 January 1941, aboard the SS *Siboney*. Her date of birth is given on the passenger manifest as 1907, her place of birth Nuremberg, her age thirty-four. Her port of departure was Lisbon.

These contemporary dates match those specified in Richard Lindner's letter to Frau Amschwand, written in Lyons on 13 February 1941, stating that his wife had arrived in New York fourteen days earlier. The date of birth doesn't match the one on Elsbeth's later application for American citizenship, but I put that – and the misspelling of Nuremberg in the application – down to sloppy bureaucracy.

This woman, then, is the Elsbeth Lindner who had married Richard, and who, after her arrest in Paris in late 1939, was incarcerated in an unidentified camp for women and released some months later, perhaps as a result of friends in the fashion industry interceding on her behalf. Elsbeth's immigration file includes a statement by her, specifying, if not the place, at least the start date of her imprisonment: 'Between May 1940 and January 1941 I was interned and then upon my release I went to Casablanca.' Another document records her residence in Casablanca as lasting from July to December 1940. It seems likely, then, that she spent some three months in detention.

Footage exists of the *Siboney*, a ship of the American Export Lines, docking at Jersey City in 1941.[1] I have scanned its three minutes, eighteen seconds of black-and-white film looking for my aunt, but cannot see her among the individuals busily descending the gangway.

As refugees go, the newsreel figures bear scant comparison with the drained and desperate folk we are accustomed to seeing nowadays on television news, crossing the Mediterranean on untrustworthy inflatables. The men and women – and a few children – reaching safety in 1941 wear hats and furs, suits and overcoats. They seem busy, sometimes happy, but essentially calm, despite having sailed away from a continent that had tried to eradicate them. Perhaps the days at sea were soothing, a thin preliminary layer of tissue laid over what had gone before.

The more specific details of Elsbeth's journey, in time and psychology, after being separated from Richard in Paris would appear to be irretrievably lost. Richard's letter to Frau Amschwand confirms that she was held in a French detention camp for some period. While several of these, like Brens and Gurs, imprisoned both men and women, only one – Rieucros, in the south-west – is known to have been a women's camp. Built to isolate members of the International Brigades (groups of Comintern-supported volunteers who fought with the Republicans during the Spanish Civil War) from the French population, it was repurposed, after war broke out, to contain 400 'suspicious and undesirable foreign women'.

Wherever Elsbeth was detained, she – like Richard, Arthur Koestler and thousands of others – suffered the misery and degradation of the appalling living conditions found in the French camps. Living quarters took the form of long wooden huts with straw for bedding that was changed rarely and was infested with vermin. Water was scarce and hygiene near impossible. It was cold and many prisoners had been unable to bring adequate clothing with them. A day's food rations consisted of 180 to 200 grams of bread, 2 to 3 grams of fat, 50 grams of rice twice weekly, turnip and swede soup, and a cup of coffee.[2] Predictably, health declined quickly in such conditions, as did morale.

Yet, somehow, people who had never previously suffered such privations came through. I have often wondered whether, in the same circumstances, I would do as well. When younger than I am now, I have speculated that I might possess the physical stamina. But thinking of my mother's elderly mother, or Julius, and feeling late middle age creeping on, I begin to doubt it, and the cruelty of such treatment – and the inhumanity it confirms – settle more oppressively in my shrinking bones.

But Elsbeth, in her early thirties, endured it, survived it and left mainland France in the second half of 1940, to reach the port of Casablanca in the French colony of Morocco.

This North African country had already contributed an astonishing 47,000 troops to the war effort.[3] After France fell, Hitler placed value on its naval bases, should an offensive be launched against North America. 'Casablanca… lay directly across from South Carolina, making it a good staging point for a German assault on the United States.'[4] But later, absorbed by the fronts against Britain and the Soviet Union, the Führer shifted his priorities, setting his interest in these bases to one side.

Meanwhile, in the summer of 1940, ships from Marseilles were ferrying large numbers desperate to quit France to Morocco. Demobilized troops were being repatriated, and refugees were fleeing. As the largest Atlantic port in Africa, Casablanca had become a refugee centre for those in flight to the Americas, not least Jews. To accommodate them, the French Protectorate established yet another internment camp, Aïn Chock, another scene of squalor and chaos. Thankfully, the Jewish community of the city stepped in to ameliorate the quality of life for hundreds who were 'morally and physically broken'.[5]

Casablanca was a way station, but the business of travelling on was complicated and laborious.

> Since the fall of France, refugees had deluged the American consulate seeking visas to immigrate to the United States. Obtaining one, however, was an involved and often lengthy process requiring applicants to fill out forms, provide documentation, obtain sponsors, show means of financial support through bank accounts or family connection, and submit to an interview and medical exam. The refugee also had to prove he or she had booked passage on a ship or airplane departing for the United States. For most refugees in Casablanca, that meant a reservation on a ship leaving Lisbon.[6]

Alone and in extremis, Elsbeth faced enormous challenges, and was possibly not in the best of health. One intriguing scrap of paper, dated 30 November 1940, written on the headed notepaper of Casablanca's Hôpital Jules Colombani, suggests that she was scheduled for some kind of medical consultation there. Another memory from one of Richard's New York friends offers the more troubling suggestion that she tried to take her own life during these months in Africa.

In whatever condition, she endured the lengthy bureaucratic process, travelled on to Lisbon, boarded the *Siboney* and made it to the New World. Her immigration file includes the question: 'How much money did you have in your possession at the time of your arrival?' The answer: 'Between two and three dollars.'

At this point, the figure of Joseph Bornstein – a member of Elsbeth and Richard's circle in Paris – needs a fuller introduction. His papers are lodged at the Center for Jewish History in New York City and run to some 1.4 linear feet, as seems appropriate for 'one of the most accomplished journalists of Weimar Germany'.[7] They include one photo, of a slim man with a wide, clear brow and penetrating gaze. His application to enter the United States, dated September 1940 and stamped Algiers, gives his height as five foot nine inches, his weight as 176 pounds and his eyes as hazel.

Born to a Russian father in Cracow, Poland, in 1899, Bornstein and his family soon moved to Germany, and he was educated in Berlin and later Vienna. Mixing with prominent German socialists in the 1920s, he became executive editor of an 'intellectual journal', the *Tagebuch*, until 1931.

Joseph Bornstein's reports and investigative work were highly prized and he was extolled as a *Wunderkind* of German journalism in an obituary in the *Aufbau*. He covered a story of the investigation and trial of the murders of German Communist leaders, Rosa Luxemburg and Karl Liebknecht, the story of Sacco and Vanzetti, and others. Joseph Bornstein was a member of the Deutsche Liga für Menschenrechte (German League for Human Rights).[8]

As an outspoken critical voice and strong opponent of right-wing and populist parties, Bornstein was one of those who knew to leave Germany instantly in 1933. In Paris, he maintained his journalistic work via *Das Neue Tagebuch*, while also contributing to other periodicals of the German exile community in France, such as *Montag Morgen* and *Pariser Tageszeitung*.

> After the war broke out Joseph Bornstein volunteered in the French army, but was interned in the camp Marolles, near Blois. In February 1940 he was mobilized in the French army, and was attached to the British Expeditionary Force in the 712th labour company. Joseph Bornstein was sent to Africa with this unit and later demobilized in September 1940. Shortly thereafter he was issued an emergency visitor visa by the consul of the United States in Algiers, Algeria. He arrived in the United States in March 1941 and settled in New York.[9]

The above account, corroborated in documents to be found in the 1.4 linear feet at the Center for Jewish History, shows Bornstein following a path not so dissimilar to Richard's. The exception is the Algerian chapter. What the papers do not include is any reference to time spent in Casablanca.

However, family mythology has it that this is where Joseph Bornstein and Elsbeth Lindner reconnected after their arrests and separate experiences at the hands of the French. And that this is where they fell in love.

Perhaps family mythology drank too deeply at the fountain of cinema. Elsbeth was not played by Ingrid Bergman, nor Joseph – or Richard – by Paul Henreid, as in the film *Casablanca*. Elsbeth did, however, make a choice, like Ilsa in the movie, between versions of love and duty. Whatever the location – pre-war France, mid-conflict North Africa – she chose Joseph.

Decades later, Richard commented on these events in an interview with John Gruen ten days before his death.

My first wife was a fellow art student at the Munich Academy. We lived together for a few years [nine to be exact], and then she fell desperately in love with a writer – a close friend of mine. She didn't exactly leave me, but she lived with the writer. It was an understood relationship – but it took a bad turn. The writer became very ill and died. And after that, my wife committed suicide.[10]

The meaning of 'an understood relationship' – to each of the parties – remains an enigma, but, more conventionally, Elsbeth and Richard were divorced in the early 1940s and she went on to marry Joseph Bornstein on 1 September 1943, her birthday. She also, for unknown reasons, took the name of Jacqueline. The New School drawings are signed 'J. E. Lindner', her professional name. In 1950 Jacqueline Elsbeth Bornstein petitioned for naturalization in the City of New York. Her date of birth was given as 1 September 1906. Her address was 155 East 77th Street. Her petition was granted.

These scant paragraphs obviously span an enormous gulf. The questions left unanswered are tormenting. When did the marriage go wrong? What did Elsbeth see in Joseph that she had not found in Richard? How had the war affected her? Was she happy, ever?

Questions about Elsbeth's psychology and emotional landscape become all the more perplexing in the light of Richard's bald and ultimately tragic statement above. Documents and correspondence in the Bornstein papers shed only a little light.

One is a single-page typewritten contract headed 'a Memorandum of Agreement entered into on the Fourteenth day of May, 1950, between Jacqueline E. Lindner-Bornstein, hereafter called "the worrier" and Joseph Bornstein, hereafter called "the anti-worrier", and concerns the future life of the two parties to this agreement'. It continues:

> In recognition of the fact that life is short and that efforts to enjoy every minute of it are of utmost importance, the Worrier and the Anti-Worrier covenant as follows.
>
> 1. The Worrier will cease worrying on signature of this agreement, and this in particular concerning the earning and spending of moneys.
>
> 2. In the future the Worrier will not [sic] longer suppress any desire to buy things or to spend money on things in which she is interested, and this at any time and on any occasion at and on which such buying and spending may contribute, and reasonably justify the expectation of contributing to her enjoyment of life.

Clause three establishes that the pair will review their finances on the first day of every month. Then:

> 4. The Worrier and the Anti-Worrier promise one another that they will be satisfied and feel comfortable as long as the examination described in the above paragraph 3 of this agreement results in the finding that the amount of cash at their disposal surpasses the sum of $6000.
>
> 5. The Anti-Worrier grants the Worrier the right to worry as much as she pleases at and from the moment of the finding that the cash at their disposal is not more or less than $6000.
>
> 6. The Anti-Worrier promises that from the moment mentioned in the above paragraph 4 of this agreement he not only will abstain from spending moneys on things which the Worrier does not declare as indispensable, but also will participate full-hearted in all worries of the Worrier and

devote all his energy to efforts of increasing his income and helping the Worrier to increase her income.

7. This agreement shall be binding upon the Worrier and the Anti-Worrier under all circumstances, in peace and in war or civil-war, in spring, summer, autumn and winter, in sunshine, rain, snowfall, thunderstorms, and any other event.[11]

It is formally signed by both parties but not witnessed.

Sweet in intention and comic in tone, this document nevertheless suggests a darker subtext of anxiety on Jacqueline/Elsbeth's part. Inevitably, money was an overpowering concern to many refugees who had been forced to abandon virtually all assets and flee. Their new homes, while safe, offered polar extremes of hospitableness and work opportunity. Yet the Lindners and Bornsteins were far from unequipped to re-establish themselves. My father found work; so did Richard, and Elsbeth, and Joseph. The New York community also offered friends and possible contacts.

Nevertheless, Jacqueline/Elsbeth was anxious enough to spur the contract, Joseph's elaborate gesture of reassurance. The same question arises here that I have considered often enough about my mother: was it the trauma of the war that made her neurotic, or was this her personality even before 1939? About both women, I am left wondering.

Probably in 1941, Joseph set off on a long trip to California, by train and sometimes car. The intention behind it seems to have been to find writing work in Hollywood – an optimistic decision, possibly encouraged by connections out west. He was living under a temporary admission visa at the time. It's therefore conceivable that his employment opportunities were limited.

During his absence, he kept up an intense and regular correspondence with Elsbeth in New York.[12] Often descriptive, it thrums with an undertone of concern and reassurance: 'Dearest,

I think of you, not without worrying. I have wished that you would regret my absence just a little, but you *promised* me that you would not be sad.'

One or two early letters are written on the Beverly House Hotel headed paper ('All Rooms With Bath'). They talk of 'our hill' – or sometimes 'our magic hill', that is, *Zauberberg*, possibly with conscious reference to the Thomas Mann novel – a place where some intense expression of commitment seems to have been shared.

Later Bornstein moved into a villa. He liked the LA lifestyle – the weather, the swimming – and tried to persuade Jacqueline/ Elsbeth to come and share it with him. He pushed her to send samples of her work, which new acquaintances could use to find studio opportunities for her. If not already acquainted with the émigré community on the West Coast, he very quickly made contact with it.

> Billie [*sic*] Wilder has treated me in a charming and touching way. Yesterday evening he invited me to dinner together with Leonhard Frank [a German writer] and Vally [unidentified] (at a funny Hollywood luxury restaurant), this morning he called me and asked if I needed money, if so I should only call him and tell him how much, this would be a natural course of action, I should not have any financial worries here... But we have not yet talked about serious matters; that should happen tomorrow, I have no idea what will happen.

Other figures – including the writers Bruno Frank, Gina Kaus and Erich Maria Remarque – play small roles in the correspondence. Bornstein hopes Remarque can help him aid 'the Spann family'. (Jews all around the world were making similar frantic efforts to aid those trapped in Europe, in the same way that Joseph, Elsbeth and Richard had been helped.) 'Yesterday I finally succeeded in getting Remarque on the phone. He promised to send money from England to Spann, I was very glad about that, and afterwards I sent him a clever "letter of thanks" which hopefully will oblige him to really do something.' Charles Spann's telegram, dated 15 September 1944, Paris, containing late congratulations to Joseph on his marriage, suggests these efforts were successful.

Jacqueline/Elsbeth's replies are lost, but are reflected in Bornstein's comments:

> My sweetheart, I received two letters from you today at the same time, the 'silly one', as you call it, and the other one, from Friday, and that was good, because otherwise I would have felt even more annoyed at myself, for writing to you in 'a way that could be misunderstood', 'in a not affectionate way', in your words. It is true that the thoughts you had were 'silly', you will be always silly if you doubt that you are *everything* to me, that I continue to love you so as I did on our hill and as you felt it there. You will be always 'silly', if you deduce that I would not love you any longer or not as much as I used to do. You must not search my letters for any signs for or against it…
>
> I swear this, so that I don't need to think about what 'effect' my letters might have on you, please, never analyse my letters again. Instead, be absolutely sure that behind the apparently most untender, most objective, most austere words there is the same feeling that you felt on our hill – is that '*entendu*' [understood]?

Again and again he expresses regret for their separation, and encouragement to her to visit him in Hollywood. He promises a better life for them there than in New York. He urges her not to succumb to depression. Elsbeth seems to have been at least partially employed at this time as a travelling companion, to a Mrs Nothmann.

There are multiple references to Africa in Bornstein's letters, including mention of Boghari, also known as Boukhari or Morand, a forced-labour camp for Spanish refugees fleeing the civil war. Under the Vichy regime it housed Jews. It seems he was demobbed there in September 1940 and perhaps waited in the camp for his visa, which was granted a few days later.

He also compares the letters he is writing now to 'those in Africa', which suggests that he and Elsbeth corresponded while she was in Casablanca and he in Algeria, and speaks of fears 'that the same as in Algiers would happen again' – this in a paragraph that refers to 'R' (Richard?).

While straining to produce creative writing that he might sell to the studios, he comes up with an idea:

> A series of stories or radio programmes came suddenly to my mind. Perhaps one could develop it, but I need help for its realization. The title would be 'How they found each other'. It would be the stories of how people, families, couples, friends, who lost each other due to the collapse in France, finally found each other.

About this poignantly relevant notion no more is heard. The last letter on file from California draws a picture of the musical evening Joseph attends at Max Reinhardt's drama school.

> Just in front of me there was Orson Welles with Dolores del Río... I saw a fabulous head, the one of the actor who had played 'Dodoworth'/'Dodsworth'/'Dodeworth'? I think his name is Houston, a wonderful chap, looking so witty that you would never take him to be an actor.

This will have been Walter Huston, father of John, who starred in the 1936 film adaptation of Sinclair Lewis's novel *Dodsworth*.

The California chapter closes and Bornstein returns to Jacqueline/Elsbeth's side in Manhattan. The couple marry, settle, work. Joseph at first takes a job at the US Office of War Information. Later he becomes a literary agent, representing foreign authors including Hermann Hesse and Alberto Moravia.

Elsbeth, meanwhile, resumes her illustrative career. In 1951 she is listed among contributors to the September issue of *Mademoiselle*.

> [She] illustrated Parisian fashion magazines until she took the last ship out before the French armistice with Germany; got to the US by way of designing dresses in Casablanca, cooking on an American farm. Now, with writer-husband Joseph Bornstein, she has a kerosene lighted, cold-water farmhouse on a Maine island: goes to New York in summer 'only when someone wants me badly'.[13]

This farmhouse was an elderly property with lovely grounds in Vinalhaven; Richard would sometimes visit the couple there.

Elsbeth's work in the magazine accompanies an article about new hairstyles designed by 'the great Michel of Helena Rubinstein's New York salon', offering blissful period hope: 'No reason, today, for a brown-haired girl to be less brightly attractive than the admittedly blessed blonde.' Her three drawings have an exquisitely simple line, depicting a Vivien Leigh-esque woman with arched brow, dark lips and bow-necked blouse. Sophistication radiates off the page.

It was, by all accounts and appearances, a happy and successful marriage, until the morning in June 1952 when Bornstein was found dead of a heart attack. As Richard reported in a letter to his friend Hermann Kesten soon after, 'Everything here is infinitely sad and hopeless. We have buried the good Joseph.'

Elsbeth had found her husband curled up in bed, as if asleep. 'He passed in his sleep. He looked strangely young and peaceful. Death was pretty good to him,' Richard commented.[14]

His sympathy for Elsbeth was intense and loyal. 'Jacqueline is thin and so pale, she is brave. It breaks one's heart.' He comments on her incomprehension at events. There is a report that he later offered to remarry her.

In another letter to Kesten, in September, Richard says that Jacqueline had spent a week in Vinalhaven. 'She is not yet very well. Above all so thin and very very sad.'[15] Later she was intending to go to California, 'to relatives', for a week. But then?

Despite multiple efforts, it has been impossible to establish the precise circumstances of Elsbeth's suicide, although it took place in the New York apartment she shared with Bornstein, since a later reference mentions the police eventually unsealing it when their routine follow-up was complete. The date of death was 21 October 1952. The death certificate cites 'visceral congestion' as the immediate cause, 'pending chemical examination', two opaque statements which leave interpretation open.

It is as if all other records have been expunged, and perhaps they were. This was not, after all, an era in which suicide was socially acceptable, even among bohemians.

Some detective work, however, has revealed Elsbeth/Jacqueline's resting place. She is buried together with her husband at Woodlawn Cemetery in the Bronx, and was interred there four days after her death. Their stone records them as Joseph Bornstein and Jacqueline Bornstein. Her evolution away from Elsbeth Lindner was complete.

Woodlawn is a vast, scenic and well-manicured cemetery, its meandering main drive punctuated with spacious monuments and mausoleums housing grandees like the Woolworths. The Bornsteins' corner, however, is obscure and very modest. Around them are rows of grave markers for Italians and Jews and Yankees who similarly expired in 1952, a few of the headstones marked by tokens of familial mourning: some faded flowers; a note to 'Dad'. The Bornsteins' stone is bare and faded with age, its inscription difficult to read. It's a banal and melancholy place, its anonymity out of keeping with the seismic events witnessed and emotions experienced by the couple it records.

Elsbeth remains an elusive figure, a familiar stranger. We have nothing in common other than a name, and yet her tragedy always haunted me, and does still. Her preoccupation and piercing sadness seem apparent even in those early photographs of a lovely, watchful face, but perhaps I freight the images with too much after-knowledge. I see her at the very least as a bridge from innocence to experience, in both her marriage and her wartime suffering.

Strength of the psychological kind is not always apparent. I witnessed my mother's unexpected reserves of endurance and fortitude during my father's near-fatal illness in 1974. Previously unsuspected mettle can emerge when required, even from individuals presumed sheltered or vulnerable. Perhaps Elsbeth too was heroic, for a while. But in the end, as a friend commented, she simply could not bear this loss.

My sister and I grew up in the care of parents whose loss and trauma were very close to the surface. Looking back now, the realization that they wanted – and dared – to start a family in 1945 takes my breath away. My sister was conceived that year and born in June 1946. I came along some five years later.

In the post-war chaos, with Europe awash with the homeless, the stateless, and all the other wrecked and displaced souls, the Red Cross made it their business to bring about some degrees of resolution, by sending letters to the survivors who could be traced, confirming – where known – the deaths of family members in concentration camps. Arthur received formal news of Julius's death in a Red Cross letter dated 31 December 1946.

Even before such final statements, however, I have to assume my parents would already have begun the work of encompassing – if not processing – the unbearable knowledge of how much their loved ones had suffered. Starting a new family in such circumstances is not merely evidence of defiance, or of the biological urge to procreate, but a gesture of tribute and atonement. We children were tasked with becoming another reason to live, in a world recently lost to madness. We needed, therefore, to be good and deserving, to live up to everyone's expectations of better.

My mother's own mother, Sibilla Levy, her two sisters and many aunts, uncles and cousins also numbered among the millions who perished. (Her father, a butcher who had fought for the Germans in World War I, had died in 1938.) My mother had received two heartbreaking short notes during the war – again via the auspices of the Red Cross, to whom she was everlastingly grateful – from Sibilla, both assuring her daughter she was well and not to worry.

My mother went to her grave thinking Sibilla had perished in Theresienstadt. The fact that Julius Lindner died there always caused me to wonder if their paths had crossed. But my mother never learned the truth that came to light after her own death – that her elderly mother had been transported further, beyond Theresienstadt, to Treblinka, and murdered there the night she arrived, in 1942. I am left wondering whether Else's measure of suffering would have been intensified by this fact. Or perhaps she had already reached her limit.

Her sister, Erna, who had remained in Aachen with their mother, is lost in history, in the wash of Jewish and other individuals who starved or succumbed to illness or were shot or fell by the wayside. She is recorded – in my mother's curlicued, German-schooled handwriting – at Jerusalem's Yad Vashem World Holocaust Remembrance Centre as having died in Lublin, Poland, but there is no proof of this.

The third Levy daughter, my aunt Clara, had left Aachen before the war, to live in Amsterdam with her Dutch husband Richard Culp. The couple went into hiding when the Germans invaded the Netherlands, but were discovered and sent to Auschwitz, where both perished. Their son Hans, however, survived to live a different fate: snatched by a Dutch family, lost for a while in a concentration camp for young children, then rescued, to grow up Dutch in the care of that family which had protected him but which subsequently denied my mother's wish to adopt him.

As an adult, Hans van den Broeke, as he was renamed by his foster parents, married, was father to two daughters and had a long career with the Dutch postal service. He was also heavily and valuably involved with his fellow child survivors of genocide, but perhaps unsurprisingly never seemed able to lay down the burden of sadness visible in his face at age two.[16]

He died on 20 May 2009.

Like characters in a Beckett play, these scattered individuals in my family found themselves in alien places, reoriented in strange ways, effectively obliged to start their lives anew. They had fought so hard to survive, and now they were committed to living on, to making some sense of what they had seen and done.

My father, twelve years older than his wife and more worldly, made her a promise: a secure future, a home, a business and two daughters (not just children, and definitely not boys). His confidence was hard to resist. He embraced the life force.

And he delivered. He worked restoring antiques, then as a dental technician, eventually opening a jewellery and watch-repair shop in Tontine Square, Hanley, one of Stoke's five towns, joining a community of other small traders. Stoke-on-Trent did have a Jewish community, but it was minuscule. The handful of other immigrant Jewish families we knew – the Dasches, the Cutners, the Posners – were non-observant, as were we.

My mother reported that she had not been welcomed by the Jewish community when she arrived in Stoke in 1939. Those were not our people.

Instead my parents were befriended by neighbours in Burslem (another of the five towns), where they had bought a small semi-detached house on Elaine Avenue. Around the corner lived the Joneses, a family with roots in mining. Stan Jones worked at Stoke town hall. Back-to-back with our garden lived the Perrys. Cecil Perry worked for an auctioneer. These and other locals accepted the heavily accented couple with the two young girls. Meals and outings were shared. At weekends we would drive out to the Derbyshire dales, often to the Manifold Valley, where we kids could wander safely by the river or in the caves, while the fathers washed their cars together and the mothers heated up meals over portable stoves. It was the fifties, life seemed eternally calm.

Yet, for all their optimism and striving, my parents were still processing terrible pain. My father experienced crippling headaches. There was a wound on his leg which – like Amfortas's in *Parsifal* – seemed never to heal and could bring on fevers. My mother, despite her application to and contentment in child-rearing, was depressed and fatalistic. 'Nobody loves me,' she would claim. Her separation anxiety, after we girls left home, expressed itself in iron expectations of constant communication and contact. When I visited her, as an adult, and got up to leave the room, she would still reflexively ask me where I was going. Her appetite for reminders that we were all present and correct, and that she was the same, was unassuageable.

Numberless pages and volumes have been devoted to the psychological analysis of post-Holocaust trauma. I was drawn to the subject myself in my thirties, grappling with a wish to understand better my parents' pain and its effect on my childhood.

I became involved with the Second Generation group in London, and attended meetings and conferences where distinctions seemed to be drawn between survivors who had endured concentration camps and those who hadn't. The hierarchy was unappealing. Did my mother's loss and darkness count for less because her path had not included imprisonment and physical as opposed to mental torture? It seemed to me like angels-on-the-head-of-a-pin sophistry.

But the group and others like it did undoubtedly perform useful work, allowing us second-gen folk to share our experiences of parents who could be obsessive or angry, mercurial or melancholy. I came to understand the notion of 'learned depression' as a response to stress; that the confusion over Jewish identity could throw up pain and uncertainty, leading to a sense of 'not belonging'. Survivors who sometimes wanted to talk about their experiences were perhaps disbelieved, or else their stories were deemed unbearable, and so they were silent, leaving the children to fantasize about events too terrible to be named or discussed.

Richard and Arthur, Elsbeth and Else were involuntary members of this haunted set. Obliged to carry their inexpressible mourning to the grave, they would speak about many things in order to avoid one subject. They and their peers included those who hadn't or couldn't mourn; whose lives had gaps; whose feelings might be buried alive; who felt phantom pain from severed roots; whose bodies would throw up mysterious actual pains; who had nightmares; or for whom random occurrences could trigger emotional outbursts.

Elsbeth lived – and eventually chose suicide – somewhere on that spectrum.

6

Arrival – 1940

'NEW York is a city of contrasts. An amazing, infinite, inspiring, shocking, beautiful, ugly, old, new city of seven million plus. Not so different, perhaps, from Main Street, but so much bigger, its contrasts so much stronger, through sheer, overwhelming numbers. It is a city of many cities.'[1] Richard Lindner arrived here on 17 March 1941, on board the SS *Bonet*.

He was forty years old, and penniless. He later said he arrived with $5 in his pocket. His life had broken in two, and yet he had, in a sense, come home. Lindner would always identify as a German and a Jew, but from now on he would be a New Yorker too. While the city could never restore his losses, it could propel him towards unimaginable substitutes.

'New York was the greatest experience of my life. New York was just as I had imagined it – exactly like that, and indeed I think it was the city of our dreams for everyone in my generation,' he said.[2] America generally and New York specifically would become essential to him, the previously unknown twin to his European origins.

> As a New Yorker, the strength of this country is... that they have no past. That's their strength... They can do everything without feeling guilty unconsciously. Europeans are unconsciously guilty of any new movement, never mind

whatever it was, there was always the guilt of the tradition. The Americans don't have that

he told John Jones in an October 1965 interview.[3]

And, in another conversation: 'New York is a new city every day.'[4] This, to a creative spirit, was like Christmas dawning each morning.

Among his future circle of friends would be the artist Ingeborg ten Haeff, a peripatetic German-born artist who lived in Brazil before moving to New York and marrying a second husband, Paul Lester Wiener, the architect and city planner who designed the US pavilion at the 1937 Paris World's Fair. Wiener and Lindner had met in pre-war Paris and it was Wiener — according to ten Haeff's third husband John Githens — who took pity on the recently arrived artist and gave him his own overcoat.[5] It seems my uncle had arrived with little more than the clothes he stood up in.

And yet,

> In March 1941 I arrived in New York, happy and grateful to the US for my rescue, ready to start a new life and curious about the world's greatest city, especially about the house where my mother was born. I soon went to look at the street which she had so often described to us children, but unfortunately neither street nor house existed any more.[6]

It was the post-Depression era, and the post-art deco one too, as was clearly flagged in the skyline and detailing of Manhattan's tallest buildings. Was Richard as magnetized by the cubism of the skyscrapers as another future friend, Saul Steinberg?

> The first thing Steinberg noticed about New York was its architecture, particularly the impact of cubism. He trained his European eye on the urban landscape and decided that the

dominant influences were 'Constructivism,' 'Cubism,' and 'Fernandlégerism'. Despite wartime rationing, restrictions, and blackouts, everything he saw or experienced left him 'in a state of utter delight.' The 'Cubist elements' that became his lifelong totems assaulted his eye everywhere he looked, and everything he saw became grist for his artistic mill, from the gleaming Chrysler Building, where 'Art Deco was merely... Cubism turned decorative,' to the sensuous plastic curves and neon-bright colors of larger-than-life jukeboxes, to women's dresses (short, to conserve fabric), shoes (usually high, with platforms and stilettos for heels), hairdos (upswept into elaborate rolls and curls), to men's neckties (large and bright, splashed on colorful zoot suits in rebellion against drab khaki uniforms). Taxis provided fascinating bursts of color in shiny enamel, particularly the sleek flowing lines of the Pontiac sedans... He marveled particularly at 'the sort of red that is obtained only on metal, many coats and lacquer, the illuminated taxi sign on top rendered even more clearly the jukebox origin of the car.' Billboards were a revelation in text and type. English as spoken by 'Noo Yawkahs' was a foreign language. The noise, dirt, traffic, confusion – everything that jumped out at his senses in the New York of 1942 was part of 'a very American world,' and in his opinion, one that was so 'very optimistic' that he had trouble assimilating it. In later years, he regretted that he had only sketched and not made 'large paintings' of all that he saw.[7]

These might equally have been the thoughts and responses of Richard Lindner. The sense impressions, the overload, the mood, the colours would dazzle and delight him – and feed into his subject-matter reservoir – just as much. And, of course, 'large paintings' of such images were exactly what Richard would go on to make – bright, outsize canvases capturing the fashions, fabric and street life, the symbols and iconography that had 'assaulted the eye' of his fellow artist.

And he would love it, the vulgarity and brassiness, the free sense of now and not then, the romance of Central Park and the immediacy of Harlem or 42nd Street. As for Saks, Macy's and other temples to consumerism, they would offer him revolving-door inspiration.

Richard had entered America on a six-month residency, 'for pleasure' according to his papers, and this would be extended for a further six months in order to arrange for formal immigration. Even though their marriage had reached some kind of conclusion, Richard and Elsbeth underwent these dealings with the Immigration and Naturalization Service together, presenting themselves as 'a family'.

Both claimed to be freelance artists, Richard spelling out in his second interview with the Immigration Service, for the extended residency, that he was selling commercial art to *Harper's Bazaar*, *Glamour*, *Town & Country* and an agency in Philadelphia. He claimed to have earned some $1,000 in the first six months.

During this time, between October 1941 and January 1942, Lindner was the subject of an FBI investigation. According to his file,

> A confidential informant had advised the Bureau that the subject was en route to the United States with a list of the Communist agents here, which he intended to deliver to the German Consul. He was searched upon his arrival in the United States, but no such list was found either on his person or in his baggage.

While the investigation into my uncle completely exonerated him — 'no evidence of espionage, and nothing detrimental to the subject's character was discovered' — there was still the long, slow, crucial process of application to be endured. Forms needed filling and rubber-stamping by notaries public; visas and alien registration numbers were required. Help came in the form of lawyers and the National Refugee Service.

(Richard had written to the attorney general in late 1941 to ask if the fact that his mother had been born in the United States and was an American would grant him citizenship. But he was informed there was 'no provision of law whereby a person born outside the United States of an American mother prior to 12 Noon, EST, May 24, 1934, acquired United States citizenship at birth through the citizenship of the mother'.)

Another element to be endured was the rigmarole of crossing the US border and coming back in again in order to achieve immigration visas. The couple presented themselves for a 'pre-examination' on Ellis Island in 1943, and then went on a trip to Buffalo, in order to cross into Windsor, Canada, for ten days. Lindner's 'Pre-Examination Border Crossing ID Card' describes him as five foot six, with grey eyes, of medium complexion, and bald. His photograph shows an unsmiling face with stoic, exhausted eyes. His application form adds that his hair is greying and that he speaks three languages: English, French and German.

For all New York's deserved reputation as a racial and cultural melting pot, its Jews had witnessed scenes of intense anti-Semitism only a handful of years before, courtesy of the German American Bund and the Christian Front. The Bund, closely allied with Germany's Nazi Party, affected swastikas, Hitler salutes and storm troopers. Its rally for 'true Americanism', held at Madison Square Garden in February 1939, was attended by some 20,000 cheering supporters.

The Christian Front had sprung from the radio broadcasts of Father Charles Coughlin, a Catholic priest. As early as 1930, Coughlin was commenting: 'We have lived to see the day that modern Shylocks have grown fat and wealthy, praised and dei-fied, because they have perpetuated the ancient crime of usury under the modern racket of statesmanship.'[8] Later in the decade, his unrepentantly corrosive views spread via a series of clubs among Irish Catholic populations in the Midwest and northeast, leading to harassment of Jews on the streets of New York and vandalism of Jewish businesses and synagogues.

Other Christians and interfaith groups came to the defence of the Jews, and action against the Christian Front by the FBI helped defuse its impact. Meanwhile the experiences, number and impact of Jewish immigrants from Hitler's Europe began to shift the argument and the perspective of some, if not all.

Despite these ignoble recent episodes, aspects of New York culture must still have seemed astonishingly Jewish to the new arrivals from Europe. Jews were confident and visible and their culture was proudly upheld. I remember my own first visit to the city, some thirty years later. The publishing business included many people I assumed to be Jewish, unlike in the UK, where it seemed that Jews in the industry were rare – though often notable, like George Weidenfeld and André Deutsch. I discovered a rapport and an acceptance in NYC that I had never encountered in England. But I also remember wincing at the sight of people and businesses airing their Jewishness without qualm. How could they take the risk?

A total of 132,000 German Jews fleeing Europe in World War II took up residence in the United States.[9] Of those who settled in New York City, 28 per cent had, by 1941, found homes in Washington Heights, on the Upper West Side, later known as 'the Fourth Reich'.[10] Twenty-four per cent chose Central Park West or West End Avenue, but my uncle headed to the Upper East Side, and would remain faithful to this quarter of the city throughout his life. His first address was at 5 East 62nd Street, where he paid a rent of $48 per month. Later there would be apartments on 96th, 71st and 69th streets. Many members of his circle of friends would live nearby, including the Lehfeldts at 94th and the Bornsteins, Joseph and Elsbeth/Jacqueline, at 77th.

Aspects of the city reminded him of the past. 'Richard Lindner discovered in New York streets "the carnival spirit of Munich".'[11] For him, as for so many of the immigrants, New York offered some sense of cultural familiarity, as well as an immense gulf.

> The Museum of Modern Art, a temple enshrining the internationalist style; the picturesque charms of Greenwich Village and Gramercy Park; the momentum of crowds in banks and department stores; the noisy enthusiasm of earlier immigrant intellectuals, now living on the Lower East Side... [The refugees] were captivated by visual novelties: elevated trains, barber poles, fire escapes. The neon advertisements had a special allure and pathos.[12]

This was the culture – in-your-face, irrepressible. But its counterpart was transience:

> As one novel attraction was succeeded by another, as notions of the new were revised almost by the hour, émigrés perceived a general obliviousness to what was really news: the events in Europe that flashed by in the iridescent alphabet on the *New York Times* tower, history reduced to a glimmering sensation.[13]

My uncle was back at the bottom of the professional ladder, older, wearier, but not devoid of resources. He brought experience, as well as European-ness, to the North American shore. There was an active commercial art market in New York – magazines, advertising, book publishing. This was all familiar terrain to a man of his pictorial gifts, and one who had established a significant reputation in Munich. The artist and collector Leo Rabkin described Richard's commercial work as 'absolutely brilliant'. As a freelance illustrator Lindner was very quickly able to earn his keep.

Soon after he arrived, he managed to sell a watercolour to *Town and Country* magazine to accompany a story about the composer Offenbach's New York debut in 1876. This image, which appeared in the October 1941 issue, bears a very strong likeness to the Offenbach watercolour which hung over the sofa in my family home, and which now hangs in my sister's house. Our version is dated Paris 1935 or 1936.

Richard's account of events goes as follows:

> On my third day in America I went to look for a job. I called on *Town and Country*, with a portrait of the Parisian composer Jacques Offenbach. I had painted it the night before, with hundreds of heads as background. The art director liked the picture, but he could see no way of using it in the magazine. Disappointed, I returned to the studio I had just rented, and in sudden anger I tore up the sheet and went to a movie. Coming home late that night, I found a telegram from *Town and Country* asking me to bring the Offenbach back in the morning.[14]

He describes spending the whole night recreating the work and trying to pass it off as the original. The art director proves that the replacement is a copy, but buys it for the magazine anyway, 'and an editor acquired the original for his private collection'.[15]

It's a colourful anecdote, if not quite what it seems. The family picture, painted several years earlier and now usefully painted once again, was in fact some kind of stock Lindner image, part of a sub-folio of useful art kept for advertising purposes, alongside sheets of character doodles. On his 1967 visit, Richard had said as much. The image was not quite a party piece, just the kind of thing a jobbing illustrator could produce to order.

Other publications, like *Fortune* and *Harper's Bazaar*, were attracted to his particular, refined talent. In an issue from that same year, *Vogue*'s 'And What's More…' column has a paragraph headed 'Soldier Artists', which goes on: 'Richard Lindner who painted the *Vogue*'s Eye-View in this issue is a German-born artist who, before the war, was well-known in London and Paris. (Some posters he did for an English piano firm were so decorative they found their way onto the walls of many smart houses in London.)'

The illustration itself – '*Vogue*'s Eye-View of the Open Road' – looks as if it could have come from another century. It depicts an early-vintage automobile driven by a bearded chauffeur, accompanied by a woman in Victorian garb topped off with a large, decorated hat. Behind them loom what might be London landmarks – the dome of St Paul's; St Bride's Church. The humour in the image suggests that this could be Lindner's work, yet little else seems strikingly characteristic, except perhaps for the elaborately decorated frame.

Its caption, however, rings a breezy note with darker wartime undertones:

> With so many of the world's roads 'Closed' – closed to traffic and progress and civilization – one looks with new eyes on the open roads of this hemisphere. Millions of miles of them stretch hospitably in all directions… This summer, you will be taking one of these roads. Which one?… Will it be the three-thousand-mile highway across the whole magnificent breadth of America?

In 1942 and '43, there are further Lindner credits, one for an illustration to accompany a caption on velvet shoes – 'Three velvet dinner-at-home slippers – just the thought of velvet is cosy…' Fashion wasn't his regular beat, but, unsurprisingly, at this point he would take up opportunities of whatever kind.

More mainstream commissions, however, would follow, including book illustrations and cover artwork. It was here that Lindner could stretch his wings, and open up his unique sensibility: romantic and surreal, witty and precise.

For Doubleday, in 1944, he supplied the cover art for A. J. Liebling's *The Road Back to Paris*. This collection of dispatches from France, England and North Africa by a correspondent for *The New Yorker* – 'A brilliant, witty and thoughtful book which reconstructs the shape of war and shows a knocked-out world getting to its feet again' – must surely have provoked some complicated memories in the artist.

The *Madame Bovary* illustrations – vertiginous, passionate and socially suggestive – also date from this period, as does the jacket for a novel by Richard's friend Hermann Kesten. A publisher as well as a writer, Kesten shared a similar history – Nuremberg-born, he had moved to Paris in 1933 and then New York during the war, where he worked with the Emergency Rescue Committee aiding refugees fleeing Europe. His book *The Twins of Nuremberg*, published by L. B. Fischer in 1946, received a review in *Harper's*: '[A] sense of tragedy mixed with quiet humor... pervade this long and absorbing story of two girl twins – actresses – and their twin children living their confused and romantic lives during the chaotic times in Germany between two wars.' There seems to have been no escape, at least professionally, for Richard from his recent European past.

In 1941, he was commissioned to illustrate an advert for Container Corporation of America and produced an ink-wash drawing entitled Eternal Summer on the Table, a seasonal fantasy of a recumbent girl, fruit and foliage, all laid out on a circular table perched on a carved pedestal, with an old-fashioned lamp at tilt above. This won a prize at the annual exhibition of the Art Directors Club of New York in 1942, the first of several he would be awarded in years to come.

Professionally, then, he was back on track, producing pen-and-ink line work that infused European elegance into New World consumerism. If his early style had melded surrealism and symbolism, fed by his years in Munich and Paris and sustained by youth, the crucible of his last two years had unsurprisingly introduced a darker thread of imagination into the mix.

In 1949, George Amberg analysed Lindner the commercial artist in an edition of *Graphis* magazine. 'He is unable and unwilling to compromise,' Amberg wrote. 'His approach to any assigned task is unorthodox and unpredictable, yet based on an acute grasp of purpose and always informed with a strange magical quality of imagination.'[16]

Even though, in later years, as a professional artist, Richard would look back dismissively on his illustrations, even exclude them from the body of his work, the connection is important. The role of commercial illustrator not only meant that he could pay his bills, but also laid down his foundations as a creative being.

Amberg, for example, goes on to highlight Lindner's precision, his elegance, intricacy, also the absence of a third dimension. Lindner's figures and fantastical creatures float in a foreground that is disconcertingly immediate. They inhabit a reality that is both identifiable and shockingly peculiar. When he began to paint, he would import these practices as a starting point, bringing aspects and perspectives of the commercial advertising world to his figures and proportions.

But what about the man? At what point did my uncle reconnect with his brother? And more importantly, when did he learn that his marriage was over?

Both Elsbeth and Maria Eisner are credited with helping engineer Richard's exit from Europe. Eisner, who was to become an important photo editor and agent, had herself made an escape from the continent in 1940 and settled in New York City. She remained a good friend to both Lindner partners, and Richard never ceased to express gratitude to her for her role in saving his life. On his 'Alien's Registration Record' — part of his application to enter the United States, dated October 1940, before he left Europe — he cited his proposed address in New York as 215 West 83rd Street, care of Maria Eisner.

Eisner went on to marry the noted gynaecologist Hans Lehfeldt, gave birth to a son in 1951 and named him Richard too. Richard Lehfeldt became Lindner's de facto godson. Lehfeldt told me that Richard was 'like family' in his parents' household, visiting regularly. But he also said that his mother was Elsbeth/Jacqueline's best friend. So the strange intimacy between Richard, Elsbeth and others around them spread wider, perhaps to the satisfaction of all parties, though I have to wonder.

What is definite is that Joseph Bornstein and Jacqueline Elsbeth Lindner were granted a licence to marry in Manhattan on 30 August 1943. We must assume Richard and Elsbeth were therefore divorced sometime during his first two years in the United States. (Elsbeth's immigration file includes mention of temporary residence at the Alamo Ranch, Reno, Nevada, in early August 1943, which suggests a possible divorce there and then.)

The support of friends must surely have been crucial for a man whose past had been traumatic and whose present was both raw and dark. Lindner had lost his wife to another man, and had no knowledge as to the whereabouts of his closest remaining relatives.

Richard was a social animal, even if he was known later for 'going through' friends. Now he found companionship and moral support amongst a larger set of displaced souls who shared language, ideas and some of the disorientation of emigration. His new circle would include not only the Bornsteins and the Lehfeldts, Paul Lester Wiener and his wife Ingeborg ten Haeff, writer Hermann Kesten and his wife Toni, but also artists René Bouché, Ilse Getz, Saul Steinberg and Hedda Sterne, and photographer Evelyn Hofer.

Ala Damaz and her husband Paul, both architects, were also members of the group. 'We were kind of a gang,' said Ala Damaz about this lively, German-speaking émigré community with its multiple, overlapping connections. (At times these could even seem incestuous, with affairs between parties.) Damaz worked for a while as Paul Wiener's assistant. Later she would decorate one of Lindner's apartments – all white, except for the red bathroom and black kitchen.

Steinberg, the renowned *New Yorker* cartoonist and artist, had tried to leave Europe on the same ship as Elsbeth, the *Siboney*, but missed the boat and was condemned to a more circuitous route to North America via Italy and the Dominican Republic. Like Richard, he was an outsider who brought a detachment to his visual commentary, the ability to explain the natives to themselves.

Lindner defined himself as a tourist:

My figures are the impressions of a tourist visiting New York. There is no one else in America who paints quite like that. I don't belong to any movement... I am a tourist on a visit to America who has to see all the sights. In this respect Saul Steinberg and I have a lot in common, we are both tourists, both arrived at much the same time, we are friends, and of course we see New York better than anyone who was born there. I am a tourist everywhere – meaning an 'observer'.[17]

In England, Arthur too was digging in. His new community was far from cosmopolitan, Stoke-on-Trent being an industrial town of no special allure, in the centre of the country. It was, however, far enough from London to escape the bombing, while its coal mines and steel plants played a valuable role in keeping the country's engines turning through the war years.

My father would have to put aside his passion for motor cars for some while, until he could once again afford to own one.

In the interim – and during the petrol-rationing years of the war – he and my mother at first got around on bicycles, later graduating to a motorbike with a sidecar. On this, they began their tradition of Sunday-afternoon excursions into the more rural surrounding counties, Derbyshire and Cheshire.

Food rationing continued for some years after the end of hostilities in 1945. Here, their continental palates lent the occasional advantage. My father had no interest in his tea ration and was happy to swap it for coffee, which both he and Else craved. He was also deft at rustling up something edible from powdered eggs, which came in tins and disgusted many other hungry consumers.

At some point before 1950, Arthur and Richard found each other again – I have no idea how – and the tradition of Richard's miraculous parcels began. One early gift, so the story goes, was of a pair of Levi jeans. My father took them to be labourer's clothes and refused to wear them. Another gift, of a large tin of marmalade, met a similarly cool response.

In the late 1940s, Arthur decided it was time to put an end to his make-do income and become his own boss. He had been repairing handbags for a shop in the centre of Hanley – the shopping Mecca of Stoke's multiple towns. When this business, known as The Lucky Bean Shop, became available, he decided to lease it and sell jewellery, mid-price items affordable to the working-class population. Mrs Day, the owner of the property – a small rectangle of ground-floor space with a tap and a gas line but no toilet facilities – also sensed an opportunity. Her terms were rent plus 50 per cent of the business's annual earnings, and so they remained from the start of the jewellery shop's life until its end, sold to a new owner in 1983.

It was an exploitative deal, but my father took it. He had never been a shopkeeper, but his instincts were sound: the site was exceptional, in Tontine Square, near a bus stop and across from the great triumvirate of British stores of the era:

Woolworth's, Marks & Spencer, and British Home Stores (later to be joined by Boots the Chemist). On one side of what became our shop was a grocery business, quaintly named Home & Colonial. It sold biscuits, butter, flour, other dry goods – all loose – and canned and packaged foods as well. Our other neighbour was a butcher, the kind with sawdust on the floor and carcasses hanging from hooks all around the perimeter. The foot traffic was tremendous.

As the decade drew to a close, both brothers found themselves in a more secure place. Arthur had a business, a family and a home. Richard had a body of commercial work and an outstanding reputation. The brothers seemed to have shared an impulse to shrug off the kinds of employment that had allowed them to start again yet limited their horizons. They wanted to redefine themselves, and their destinies. Arthur had made his risky moves into home and business ownership in the later years of the decade. Richard's timing was similar. As 1950 began, and he approached his fiftieth birthday, he was ready to step away from the relatively safe shores of freelance commercial art. The urge to lose himself in his own creativity had become irresistible. He would give himself some time and space away from the New York round, to see what would emerge.

7

Evelyn and the Letters

EVELYN Hofer was a member of Richard's American émigré circle and an artist in her own right. Art critic Hilton Kramer called her 'the most famous unknown photographer in America'.

She was also one of the core group of women – including his sister, his mother and his two wives – whose roles were abiding and fundamental to the artist. Hofer's particular functions included mentee, confidante, partner, cook and companion.

Small and sprightly, Evelyn was born in Germany in 1922, in the small south-western town of Marburg an der Lahn, in Hesse. As the Nazis came to power, her family – who were not Jewish – fled to Switzerland and then Spain, but the civil war forced them back to Switzerland. In common with Richard, Evelyn trained, in her early years, for a career as a classical pianist, and applied to study at the conservatory in Paris (in the class of Alfred Cortot). But she was not accepted and attended the École Internationale in Geneva instead.

Becoming interested in photography, she started private lessons with Hans Finsler, an influential teacher and photographer at the Zurich *Kunstgewerbeschule*, and then went to Basel to be apprenticed to Robert Spreng. Later, she returned to Studio Bettina in Zurich to learn the operation of the Leica camera.

In 1942, the family decided to abandon Europe completely and moved to Mexico City, by way of Casablanca. Here, Evelyn gained Mexican citizenship.

Young and female, searching for freelance work in Mexico City, she met some barriers: 'I encountered so much opposition because I was a woman that I couldn't get assignments,' she recalled. 'But I was determined to be a photographer and no amount of Latin parochialism was going to stop me.'[1]

Arriving in New York in 1946, her commitment to a career in photography remained strong, and found a response at *Harper's Bazaar* where the art director Alexey Brodovitch hired her. She would go on to spend three years as a fashion photographer, a sector she grew to hate, yearning instead to photograph everyday life and people. Her opportunity came in the mid 1950s, when she was invited to supply the photographs to illustrate Mary McCarthy's book *The Stones of Florence*, published in 1959.

The impressive results and Evelyn's knowledge and understanding of European culture led to collaboration with other authors, such as V. S. Pritchett and Jan (James) Morris, and work on books on London, Spain, New York, Washington DC and Dublin. She also worked on a book about Paris, which, for unknown reasons, was never published.

During one of her working trips to London, she met a fellow photographer, younger than her, an Englishman named Humphrey Sutton. Evelyn and Humphrey married in 1962 and were divorced in 1978. With her marriage to Sutton she acquired British citizenship, and went on to use her British passport most of the time. Unlike many of her friends she never applied for US citizenship.

But her relationship with Richard flowed like a current through, under or alongside all these events, and is mirrored in a decades-long flow of correspondence. His role in *her* life was as partner, friend, mentor, fellow cat-lover. Evelyn would credit Richard with playing a major role in her work. 'He influenced me tremendously... he showed me how to look.' And she claimed to owe him her 'universal eye', seeing, in nature, a photograph much the way an artist would see a painting.

Lindner said of Hofer:

What fascinates me about Evelyn's work is that she does portraits of everything; be it a tree, be it a human being, or be
it a chair. It's always a portrait. She does not see things only
as objects; the object becomes a dramatic experience. She
has a poetic and romantic approach and a certain innocence;
she is truly a poet.[2]

He told *her* she was the only one who understood him, and that
perhaps he had woken up her talent, as she had done for him.

They met in 1947. 'I was introduced to René Bouché and
René introduced me to Richard and we fell in love.' She
encouraged Lindner to paint, holding his early work to be his
finest. The length of their romantic relationship is unclear.
But even when it was over, the attachment continued, solid
and sustaining. It survived differences of opinion. For example, Evelyn found great peace and resolution through her
commitment to Jungian analytical psychology. She would say
that Jung 'saved my life'. Richard, however, had little time
for psychiatric or therapeutic analysis. Perhaps this related to
his feelings about genius and madness, in connection with
Prinzhorn. Or perhaps, as Evelyn posited, Lindner – like his
close friend Steinberg – feared that any attempt to understand
the psyche better would have a countervailing destructive
influence on the art.

Evelyn knew Richard as well as anyone did, and believed
in him and his talent, which she said defied classification or
categorization. But she could be salty, too, in her opinions. For
example, in her view Richard said a lot of stupid things about
his own work.

The connection also survived Richard's second marriage,
despite Evelyn's less than approving feelings towards the second

Mrs Lindner. According to John Githens, Richard was due to have dinner at Evelyn's apartment, along with Githens and Ingeborg ten Haeff, on the night of his death.

Richard died in 1978. Evelyn, twenty-one years younger, outlived him by three decades; she died in Mexico City in 2009. Her estate included a cache of correspondence between the couple, dating from the early 1940s through to the 1970s. There are a great many postcards, many hand-tinted European scenes, some comical, some with added illustrations by Richard, introducing himself into the picture. Quite a few are of kittens.

The largest tranche of the correspondence comes in the form of letters written by Richard to Evelyn during the crucial six months in 1950 when he left New York for Paris, intending to focus exclusively on painting there, to shed the role of commercial illustrator and emerge as an artist.

Of all the research material available – the scholarly work, the newspaper cuttings, the reminiscences and interviews – these letters offer the best insight I have yet uncovered into Richard. While written to a lover at perhaps the height of their involvement, accompanied by whatever layers of attachment and concealment that might apply in such circumstances, they are also the closest I have come to his voice.

They start off in a rush of frequency as Richard leaves New York for Europe, excited and nervous, then slow down as he settles into his temporary Parisian home and begins to fulfil his creative aspirations. Richard's style is fluid, with sentences often running together without punctuation, ranging swiftly from topic to topic within a fairly confined range. He talks to Evelyn mainly in German, but smatterings of English and French creep in.

The tone is sometimes agitated – as when he asks her to help secure the lease on his New York apartment – sometimes protective ('I worry a lot about you') and often fond. The pages are strewn with caricatures of himself, although verbal jokes are rare.

This is the correspondence of a man taking an enormous gamble, finding comfort in sharing the circumstances of his risk. Richard was single, free of dependants and professionally secure at the time. But he had not been fulfilling the self he discerned himself to be. In his head he was a painter, and that sense, accompanied by a long mental gestation, was finally to be indulged, if possible released. At the age of forty-nine, it was undoubtedly a risk worth taking. Nevertheless, his decision, as well as the physical nature of disrupting his life in order to redefine himself, was undeniably bold.

Why do this in Paris, rather than on Long Island, or in upstate New York, where friends had country homes? Richard was nine years into his new life in the United States in 1950, but, in spite of everything, Europe quite possibly felt more like his natural home, as it did for my parents. Not Germany, never again Germany, but Paris where, despite pre-war professional frustrations and deepening shadows, Richard had relished all kinds of creative associations and stimuli. Perhaps it was simply that distance would help. Or perhaps because something radical was essential to the whole undertaking.

Richard booked himself a passage for April 1950 on RMS *Queen Mary*, a ship of the Cunard Line that made a regular, twice-weekly run between New York and Southampton. For a man who always seemed to fret about money, it was an interesting decision to travel first class.

Despite the comfort, however, his account of the journey includes many grumbles. The weather is bad, the company patchy, the speed slow. At one point he sees a plane flying overhead, in the direction of England, which compares unfavourably with the ship's rate of knots. Why, then, did he choose to travel by sea? Because that was how he had arrived in the

United States a decade earlier? Because he was carrying a lot of art equipment? To allow the transition back to Old Europe to take place at a gradual pace?

Whatever the explanation, he arrived in Southampton on 22 April 1950. It was his first ever visit to England, and his first return to Western Europe since 1941, a turning back of the cultural clock that seems to have caught him unprepared. Strolling the city with the *Queen Mary*'s radio operator, Richard was affected and shocked by what he saw. 'The city was pretty much bombed out. Ruins.' People were limping, or missing limbs. They were poor, their clothes cheap: 'the war is still in their faces.' Yet, 'round the park it's pretty, there are flowers, and they have the trees that I'd forgotten.' His American passport made him feel ashamed. Paris, he hoped, would not be like that.

Another ship ferried him on to Le Havre; presumably he took a train from there to Paris, where decisions about his accommodation were still up in the air. Would it be the Hôtel Perreyve in the Latin Quarter, or somewhere else that Alexandre Alexandre would find? He was missing his New York friends and doubting himself. This trip was a crazy idea, he blurts.

But it wasn't. And soon he found his feet.

For all the reports by friends and colleagues over the years that Richard was delightful and congenial company, the letters reveal a man whose social self was variable. Friends seem to be important, essential even, but they also give rise to an enormous, mercurial range of critical comment. Sometimes – as in the case of his brother – Richard could be warmly appreciative one day, waspish another.

Arthur phoned Richard during the Paris period, inviting him to visit England, telling him there was a room ready in his home, offering cash, of which he said he had plenty. (This was not entirely true, but he had enough.) Richard writes warmly to Evelyn about his brother: 'He was always generous, even when he had no money.' A moment of nostalgia takes over: 'He's a really nice bloke and grew up with me.' But later, when an eight-day visit by Arthur, Else and their daughter is on the horizon, Richard is derisive – 'You might well laugh' – and clearly dreading the experience: 'They will make me so anxious. I'll need a break afterwards.'

This is not the only instance of a push-me-pull-you attitude to a member of his circle. Friends might be liked even if their art is dismissed. On another occasion a female friend is described as 'disgusting' and yet Richard admits he doesn't want to stop seeing her. He has even told her how he feels. 'It seems most people love to hear the truth from me.'

The sense emerges of a man with clearly defined limits. His appetite for engagement is real and deep, but it exists alongside crisply judgemental opinions, and another essential: the need for withdrawal and creative space. Impatience for the latter, and a refusal to waste time in unsatisfactory company or places, recur regularly, like a chiming clock.

Nevertheless, for all the privately or publicly expressed testiness, Richard's circle was sizeable. The letters are littered with the names of friends with whom Richard spends time in Paris, more than two dozen of them, some couples, some visitors from the United States or other countries. He clearly wants to receive or accompany them, dine with them, talk of art, even gossip about mutual acquaintances. Yet the mentions often arrive hand in hand with a swipe. The result is a list of epithets longer than the list of acquaintances. Boring, superficial, petty, reactionary, bourgeois, tasteless, stupid: these are the judgements that crop up most often.

There's a suggestion of misanthropy here. The stupid chatter he hears on the streets of Paris helps Richard feel glad to withdraw and work. Cats have more charm than people. 'People bore me even if they are not boring.'

Evelyn, however, is set apart. She is his 'Goldbaby', his Chanel Number Five, the recipient of millions of kisses. He needs her; he is no good without her; he wants to share all his thoughts on art and all his experiences in France with her. She is the only one who understands him.

But two decades separate them, and a great deal of creative experience. Evelyn's gratitude for Richard's influence has been mentioned, but, as experienced in the letters, it comes over at times with a parental or even patronizing tone. Perhaps it didn't matter, or perhaps the strength of her feelings and regard for Lindner's abilities and insights softened the edge.

They also have a cat in common, Puck, which had been a gift to Richard when the kitten was two months old. 'Completely black, even the whiskers... with a little mouth [that] is also black. A "he", naturally, he is charming and affectionate.'[3] Puck seems to have been placed in Evelyn's care for the duration of his owner's absence.

When Evelyn sends Richard a photograph of Puck, his response is pure delight at the sight of his pet, but also at the quality of her art: 'Everything is first class – the composition, the values, the spirit... really clean and artistic work.' A photo of Evelyn is pinned to the wall of Richard's hotel room which doubles as his studio. There's a place for the photo of Puck nearby. Now, he says, the family is complete.

Arriving in Paris in late April, Richard quickly adopts a lifestyle that seems comfortably reminiscent of his earlier time spent there. Letters are written from Café de Flore, from Les Deux Magots, from a little cafe on Boulevard Montparnasse. He describes his daily regime: breakfast is black coffee and two croissants bought and consumed at a bistro close to his Left Bank hotel, where he is greeted as *l'Américain*. The meal is over by 8.30. Lunch, at 1.30, is cheese (brie), three bread rolls and a quarter-litre of red wine. Then it's back to work till four. Dinner may be eaten alone or in company. Bedtime is around eleven, which, he explains, is the Parisian hour for sleep.

The intervening time is devoted to work. Richard applies himself with all the single-minded intensity appropriate to this six-month suspension from normal life. He describes himself working at a furious rate and tells Evelyn: 'I've painted more than two pictures in a month. If I didn't have to stop fourteen days beforehand, to let things dry, I could have painted ten.' In a postcard to Saul Steinberg dated the end of May, he says: 'I have finished already three paintings,' while wishing his friend a pleasant summer.

Particular works are mentioned – *The Academician, The Wunderkind, A Portrait of Verlaine* – but the amazing outpouring, clear evidence of the mental preparation that preceded it, of his readiness, is accompanied by revealing commentary: 'I'm just as critical of myself as before. But I'm convinced that I'm talented, something I've often doubted, as you know. I can see it better because I've never before been so uninterrupted.'

Through responses to and advice about Evelyn's work, which she seems often to have sent with her letters, Richard discusses aspects of his philosophy of art. 'You can never seek the new, only find it.' New directions are born of time and circumstance. If you embark on something different – in Hofer's case, experiments with colour photography – do more, and don't stop or you will be frightened. New things must be repeated until one feels secure. Experience is everything.

When not working, confronting his own demons, experimenting with colour himself – a subject which seems to fascinate him – Richard immerses himself in culture: films, art exhibitions, theatre visits. He goes to the Modern Art Museum at the Trocadéro and glories in the Picasso and Matisse room. He's excited about an exhibition of Yugoslav primitive frescos, and even more so by a show of masters from Cologne, including an outstanding self-portrait by Dürer at the age of about twenty. '*Quelle beauté*. What a master he was, even then... How poor and unimaginative we are today in comparison.'

Movies watched include *Berliner Ballade* and Cocteau's *Les Enfants terribles*. But it's a visit to the Circus Medrano that excites Lindner as much as anything. This Parisian institution was long a haunt of artists and intellectuals – 'Toulouse Lautrec did all his circus paintings there and everything is unchanged' – and its legendary clowns, the Fratellini Brothers, had been the star performers since the 1920s. When Richard visits, the entertainment is sparsely attended and the few audience members are elderly, like the performers. But Richard is full of admiration for the Fratellinis' style, their balletic movement and art of pantomime. He even admires the beauty and taste of their costumes. But their commitment strikes a special chord: 'You have to respect them for knowing their métier.' This, for Richard, is among the highest of compliments.

In Paris, in 1931, he had been commissioned to illustrate Grock's *Life's a Lark*, the biography of an earlier Medrano clown who had made his first appearance at the circus in 1908 and went on to massive success. Later, in 1935, Richard had painted a watercolour entitled *Grock et Fratellini*, a work which at some point found its way into my father's possession and hung in our family home, perpetually scaring the bejeezus out of me. Perhaps memories of these illustrations and their associated era resurfaced during this post-war circus visit. But also, popular culture generally and circus entertainers specifically were constants in Richard's *oeuvre*, and in the paintings to come there would be roles for jugglers, pimps, ringmasters, performers and Coney Island too. Distraction, entertainment, spectacle belonged in Lindner's symbolic storehouse, freighted less with joyous and heady excitement, and more with perplexing and mysterious nuance, threat and alienation.

★

The meeting between Arthur and Richard – their first face-to-face encounter since the mid 1930s – seems to have taken place around May. For Richard, it felt like something of an invasion. His comments to Evelyn suggest that he looked on his brother and family rather as he had his parents. They were bourgeois and conventional, also fussily over-attentive towards my sister, now four years old and a reluctant walker who was insisting on being wheeled in a pushchair as much as possible.

Other details of the visit are scant. Did the brothers argue this time as well, or was the horror story of their father's death, whether discussed or not, enough to tamp down long-held differences of opinion?

According to the art dealer Nancy Schwartz, Richard never spoke about Arthur, forming in her mind an impression of some massive rift. The postcards and the parcels exchanged between the pair contradicted that assumption, as did Richard's more positive asides, and yet there could have been so much more contact. Were the brothers as far apart in 1950 as previously? Farther? Were their separate choices, made fifteen years earlier in the same city – to go back, to stay – reappraised? Why, a year after this meeting, did my parents choose to name me after Richard's ex-wife, surely at the very least a provocative choice?

The six months seem to pass relatively quickly, with Richard's moods flickering between excitement and detachment, gossip and routine, art theory and the mundane, much of it connected by observation of the French and the tourists around him: Paris is cheap. The best theatre tickets only cost $2. A three-course meal, with wine, cover and service, amounts to 240 francs, or 90 US cents. He likes the rain better in this city, and the bells, and the empty streets. He has had a haircut. Some girls in a cafe take him for a French artist.

It's Europe, fascinating, familiar, although also redolent of events in the not-so-distant past. There's an influx of German tourists in Paris, he observes, and the locals cater to them, with German books in the bookshops. Contact with Arthur reminds Richard where he is from. But the French have started to forget. On Bastille Day, he hangs out on the streets, watching 'real people, their faces unchanged since the Revolution'. Music is playing, old French chansons like 'Sous les toits de Paris'. He buys the sheet music, then sees it was printed in Germany. 'There's no hatred towards our Fatherland,' he comments. 'It falls ever further into the past.' But not necessarily for those like him, or Evelyn, or Arthur and Else.

The final letter from this pivotal period, dated 14 August 1950, is written late one night, after dinner, at a cafe table, with the city deserted for the annual summer break. It's an evocative portrait of Paris – very still, just a few cats running around, the streets scarcely lit. The shops are shut, Richard reports, and art supplies difficult to find. The bakers take it in turn to close in various quarters and he must walk distances for his morning croissants. Restaurants, cafes and cinemas are shuttered too, and the tourists have taken over the city. Yet Richard is happy. 'It's like being in an empty flat.'

He has had invitations to go to the mountains, but 'I decided to spend these four weeks here and paint two more pictures. Who knows when I'll return.' He is convinced he will be bringing a lot of good stuff back to New York, enough for an exhibition.

Then the conversation shifts to Evelyn's work, more encouragement, laced with a little criticism: 'The photo with the stockings I don't like.' But she has helped secure the lease for his flat and he is grateful. He will be home in six weeks.

Later he would comment, 'I went back to Paris for half a year, and that trip was my "goodbye" to Europe. I found that you do not become an American in America, but by going back to Europe.' Was this one of the 'stupid things' specified by Evelyn? Lindner rightly claimed this period was a watershed.

But it had not burned his origins out of him. They would never be eradicated; he could wring an essence out of them, press them into service.

A year later, the tables have turned. Evelyn is working abroad, in Paris, also Istanbul, Beirut and later Rome, and Richard is the one back in New York City, now helping her out with domestic and financial matters, as she had for him. She is still his Goldbaby and his support and concern for her are evident, yet some of the early intensity between them seems to have faded. Nevertheless a long gap in Evelyn's responses gives rise to uncertainty on his part, and the possibility that she is involved with someone else.

This smaller batch of letters from 1951 – all typed – begins during the summer. Richard is still juggling commercial work alongside his painting, including illustrations for *Charm* ('The Magazine for Women Who Work') and *Town & Country*. Drily, he comments: 'It seems that as an illustrator I'm currently in fashion.' His ambition to be redefined as an artist is almost palpable. He feels pinched for time and although needing to make a living, he resents not being able to give all his attention to his art, especially 'just now, when I begin to see and understand a lot, but that's how it goes with all creative people, especially those who develop late'.

Meanwhile, the city is stifling and many friends have left for the country. Richard takes up an invitation to spend five days in East Hampton, with René Bouché, who has rented (Robert?) Motherwell's house. (If Richard really did visit Robert Motherwell's house, he had a view of an architectural gem now lost to history. It was one of only two homes built by the French architect Pierre Chareau, and was a striking, glazed, Quonset-hut shaped structure that doubled as a studio. It was later torn down.)

He enjoys the trip, would like to repeat it; his hosts were very nice, and there was an opportunity to visit Jackson Pollock, whose behaviour appalled Richard – stupid when sober, beastly when drunk – as did his technique, which he finds ridiculous. Pollock is now in the post-drip phase, trying to find a balance between abstraction and the figurative. Richard describes the artist painting large canvases full of black-and-white heads, 'seemingly plan-less, hoping to get something by chance. Then he takes a knife and cuts the best bits out so they can be photographed.' The contrast between Pollock's free-form impulsiveness and Richard's fastidiousness couldn't be starker.

Although some of these summer letters are undated, the earliest must derive from the beginning of July 1951, since my own birth makes an appearance: 'I'm an uncle for the second time. Another girl. The telegram came yesterday. I'm happy for my brother.'

But the next letter sees a mood swing, after another weekend with Bouché. 'It was fairly boring.' The weather is hot both in the city and on Long Island, so my uncle came home. 'Better to sweat alone than in tedious company.'

Other friends are away too, and he has visited some of them, grousing the while. 'How boring it all is.' But he speaks warmly of the Bornsteins' farmhouse on an island in Maine, a beautiful home with lovely grounds. 'It does me good after all the fuss here.' Still, he needs to work, and would rather paint than travel.

The discussion of art continues between Evelyn and Richard, and his opinions remain robust. On the subject of Manet: 'He is inconsequential… he has nothing to say. Everything is empty and decorative. I never valued him.' Instead he extols the naive paintings of Bombois and Rousseau. And Chagall is great too, next to Klee the most poetic, although 'sadly later he was often too sweet with his colours'.

They discuss Sartre as well, and a photographic book, *Paris des rêves*, in which Richard had expressed interest and which Evelyn sends. He enjoys it but prefers Brassaï and Bill Brandt. Characteristically, he searches for personality and depth in the work and comes up short. A collection of nice photos doesn't make a book, he asserts. One has to have an idea or a thought or a theme, like 'Paris is a lonely town'. 'With a theme like that one has to some extent a structure to build on.'

Evelyn's photos, however, he finds wonderful. It's like his own work, he says – slowly everything emerges. 'How well I know it from myself.' He praises the poetry, the beauty, the use of colour, the composition. 'BRAVO!' There's a note of pride here, but pedagogy creeps in too. Did Evelyn always enjoy the instructions and critiques? She is advised, for example, to have her Leica always at the ready and to change hotels often, as the views from different rooms can be unbelievable.

Similarly, he offers rules on how to look at art – not to spend too much time looking at the paintings you like but to investigate the details of what seems special about an individual picture. Then look at those details – the colour, composition, surroundings, technique, texture – and finally take an overview of the whole work. Then leave and look at nothing else. You can quietly forget it. It will come back sometime, like a melody one suddenly begins to whistle without knowing why.

Familiar topics take their turn – gossip about mutual friends, their affairs and marital tensions. Money, culture, creativity and ambition: 'I must hit the jackpot, but how?'

Richard's birthday rolls around. He is fifty, not unhappy about the age, which he doesn't feel, but disappointed in his fifty-year-old body and sorry not to be with Evi. It's their first birthday apart. He will celebrate by taking himself to the movies. 'Perhaps I'll be a more important painter at sixty.'

But then Evelyn's surprises arrive, a telegram and a bouquet of roses, and he is thrilled. 'You must really love me.' The gifts throw him into a pensive phase about their relationship, about how well they get on, their mutual concerns, the way that each understands the other better than anyone else. 'We've never fought, we think the same, just the stupid bed.' There follows a proposal of a kind: 'If you come back single, I can't see any reason why we shouldn't stay together. So you'd better find a boyfriend or you'll be coming back to the fifty-year-old guy.'

Then again, another, undated later from this group suggests once more that the relationship is not necessarily progressing. 'When you return I've already decided we'll be good friends.' Who rebuffed whom isn't clear. Or why.

Does the explanation lie in another letter, one that takes a philosophical turn, in response to Richard discerning that Evelyn herself doesn't seem happy? He thinks she expects too much of life while he believes in destiny, that life is a gamble, with the occasional enjoyable surprise. 'I won't say that I am a happy man, definitely not. I'm just as lost and lonely as you.' But such is the human lot. Happiness is brief, peace available only on the best days. 'It's an ongoing back-and-forth. The worst is when one is satisfied. I find that the most immature and most frustrating state.' He urges her to take things a little more lightly. For his part, life seems full and rich, not least because of the feelings between the two of them.

Inevitably, perhaps, after a statement of such encouragement and the recommendation to take a brighter view, clouds amass overhead. The last two full letters between the couple are written in the aftermath of Elsbeth/Jacqueline's suicide, in December 1952 and January 1953.

In the first, Christmas has arrived, with its ritual celebrations that are progressing as if nothing had changed. People are coming and going, a friend has an exhibition – 'Nothing bad, but he has nothing to say.' Richard himself has nothing to report – a frequent comment of his. He and Evelyn have already discussed the shocking event, and: 'You had everything right and clear in your last letter. There's no point in talking of it any more. I think I've already talked too much about it, which really isn't my way.'

He has tried to get away to Haiti over Christmas, to be somewhere else, but couldn't get a flight so is staying at home and painting. (He is starting the work that will become *The Billiard*.) The Pratt Institute will be open again in early January, bringing the distraction of teaching. And he will be very happy simply to have Evelyn back. 'There will be no more craziness and all will be well. I just want to tell you that I expect nothing. Perhaps that will make the journey easier.'

In mid January, after a trip away together, the relationship seems more certain. Meanwhile friends are being thoughtful, sending notes, acting surprisingly. 'Steinberg kissed me when I visited him. What do you think of that? I would never have thought it of him.' And the police have reopened the apartment where Elsbeth/Jacqueline ended her life. It's high time for Evelyn to return.

The remaining correspondence takes the form of postcards, drifts of them written almost daily, in a tiny hand at cafe tables in France and Italy, many dating from another trip in 1956. Again, Richard has shifted to Europe for the summer, and set himself up to paint in Paris. The city seems to enable his creativity and yet he has mixed feelings about it, sometimes finding it hateful. (A postcard to painter friend Frederick Kiesler from this same period is indicative: 'It's raining. It's cold. The exhibitions are boring. I think of you often.')

On another occasion the place floods him with nostalgia, as he eats in a bistro where he had sat twenty years earlier. The capital is unchanged, yet his own life has been stacked with alteration – America, Jacqueline/Elsbeth's death, Evelyn, his new identity as a painter.

There are the usual accounts of friends met, enjoyed, disapproved of. And art gossip: Jackson Pollock's death – drunk, in a car crash – occurs that August. Richard makes his escape for a while, travelling to Italy, sometimes alone, sometimes with friends. He adores Rome, could imagine living there with Evelyn. He loves Italian food, the chaos, the easy-going population. But it's very hot and the tourists are horrible. The Sistine Chapel is a madhouse, the French and German tourists the worst.

Arthur would have agreed with his brother about Italy. He loved the country too, for similar reasons, and he too fell in love with the architecture and the glorious coastline below Naples. But Arthur was busy back in England, and didn't know his brother was in Europe. And Richard wasn't going to tell him – something about which he admits to feeling a little discomfort.

Returning to Paris, Richard agrees the Italian trip was just the break from routine – of work, cafe, cinema – that he needed. He will be back in New York in September. He has finished a painting. And yet he sounds lonely.

Now the dates on the postcards move forward more quickly, as Richard's professional life and social transition begin to gather pace. In a note to Evelyn while she is away in Spain in 1962, he admits how much he misses her. 'You are the last and nearest of my family. No one is as close and important to me as you.' It's a valediction of a kind, since soon the cards will be addressed to Mrs Evelyn Hofer-Sutton. Richard appears to like her husband, Humphrey, or at least says he does. But the gaps between the cards become wider and in 1967 he is using the same sign-off to Evelyn as he did to Arthur – 'Uncle Richard'.

The last ones are written as the sixties move into the seventies. And they are written as 'we', with Richard signing off for his wife Denise as well as himself. The couple are travelling. Richard is preparing for his big, crowning show in Paris in 1973. Evelyn is invited. It's not clear whether she went.

With the end of the correspondence, the window into Richard's daily preoccupations, struggles and opinions closes again. But we know that Evelyn stayed with him, if not as a partner, then as a keeper of his truths, and his secrets, growing out of the role of pupil into that of supporter, and occasional critic: she thought that in his late work his colours became much more crass.

The couple seem to have enjoyed a mutual loyalty, although this did not prevent Evelyn from making subjective yet informed observations about Richard's sexuality, pointing out a long phase of celibacy in his first marriage and perhaps an excessive attachment to his sister. Presumably she knew whereof she spoke when it came to 'the stupid bed'. Certainly few were likely to know better.

8

The 1950s

THERE would be no next generation for Richard Lindner. 'He was never going to have any children,' his quasi-godson Richard Lehfeldt told me. How did he know, I asked Lehfeldt? Apparently it was self-evident. And Lindner's passing remarks in letters suggested little patience for parenthood – too fussy, boring.

His focus was inward. He desperately wanted to succeed, for the money and the freedom, but mainly for the fulfilment of his self-belief: that he was not a commercial artist but a properly creative being. His letters suggest a very clear distinction in his mind between the truly artistic elite and the rest – those with just a scrap of talent, mediocrities. Evelyn and he were members of the former group.

And Paris had opened up the path. The sharp division of his six-month sojourn, and the work done there, both concrete and conceptual, fed into a confirming energy. In a 1951 letter to Evelyn, he talks of feeling grown up with regard to his paintings: 'Which means I begin to say important things in the pictures, and to express myself in poetic senses.'

Previously an illustrator for hire, whose scale was often pinpoint and minuscule, or else a watercolourist, he was now a painter in oils, working on large-scale canvases, their spaces dominated by substantial figures which would evolve into a new race of giants. He had reported a furious rate of accomplishment while in Europe, but the fruits can only be seen in a handful of paintings – one of a child prodigy, one of a corseted woman, and two portraits of French authors.

Richard was not known to be a bookish person. According to collectors and friends Leo and Dorothy Rabkin, he was totally visual. However, the writers Paul Verlaine and Marcel Proust seem to have spoken to him, both literary pioneers, both outcasts. Critics have suggested Lindner's interest lay in issues of cultural identity, and that in particular his visual exploration of time and memory would connect him to Proust's immense *À la recherche du temps perdu*.

The portrait of Proust, begun in Paris but completed in New York, has a sickly *fin de siècle* tonality. The writer, in a head-and-shoulders image and wearing a constricting collar, is hollow-eyed and haunted. The Verlaine portrait shows the artist edging

more clearly towards his iconic, full-figure imagery. Lindner attempted this portrait several times, destroying some of his efforts. The surviving image reveals a hulking man with a fearsome expression, his arms hanging awkwardly. It's a thumping representation, delivered with more ferocity and less sensitivity than that of Proust. Lindner's attraction to Verlaine was perhaps explained by the Frenchman's interest in Kaspar Hauser, a figure of Nuremberg legend whom Lindner claimed had been very important for him (as he has been to multiple writers and creative people). Verlaine had been instrumental in introducing this myth – of a possible prince, kept like an animal until his teens, then freed and humanized, and finally mysteriously murdered – into the popular imagination, through the verse/song he wrote, 'Gaspard Hauser chante', published in 1880. It was another parable of the outsider.

Through 1950 and 1951, the paintings began to accumulate. *Anna (Woman in Corset)* takes the Parisian corseted figure one stage further, peeling away distractions to deliver an immense figure with fixed gaze, Pre-Raphaelite hair and complex, one-dimensional underwear dividing her symmetrical, hoisted breasts from her pale thighs. As previously mentioned, the corseted woman was to become an essential Lindner character, a portmanteau image importing a web of content ranging across history, culture and sexuality. *Anna* is also an early example of Lindner's fleshy creatures, pale of limb and face, but rounded and plump. These figures' eyes, ears, fingers, hair, breasts and attire are painted in fine detail, and their poses, often against dark interior backgrounds, are lent colour through the detail of clothing or toys or complex patterns involving wheels, hoops and playing cards. *The Gambler*, dating from the same era, seems transitional, less of a giant, but still strongly corporeal, seen naked, in profile, within ellipses and against a background devised of games and playing-card symbols.

Art critics trace the mechanistic nature of Richard's figures to his admiration for Fernand Léger and Oskar Schlemmer. As he told Nancy Schwartz:

> Schlemmer influenced me most in the simplicity and precision which he used in his figures. Basically, he used only four shapes, the circle, the oval, the triangle and the square... It was a serious conception – you could not... make any facile exits. Of course, it was very German – you must go all the way – concentration to the utmost.[1]

The oversized *Wunderkind* children, 'monstrous freaks of nature', as Zilczer calls them, were also developed at this early stage. They can be interpreted as representatives of a timeless childhood, or possibly an early twentieth-century one, given their knickerbockers and sailor dresses. They also connect to the artist's fascination with criminality, madness and genius. Circus characters, gangsters, games of chance, toys, mysterious visitors and presences appear often in the Lindner repertoire, sharing a mood of otherness, a sense of a parallel universe in which these exquisitely realized figures interact or overlap in a preoccupied silence.

In England, for Arthur, consolidation of a more traditional kind was taking place – I, his second child, was born in July 1951. He was in his late forties, not exactly a young parent, but he was confident in his energies. Confident generally.

Long-held grievances played no part in his definition of the role of parent. At his best he was a generous and imaginative father, the playful, stable yin to my mother's more tense and unpredictable yang. His nurturing style bespoke a contented childhood, despite Richard's differing interpretation of the same circumstances. Arthur was generous, but also brought a kind of grounded – if undeniably patriarchal – discipline. He liked to spring small surprises, sometimes hiding gifts in his briefcase, not so different perhaps from the uncle he recalled who arrived with chocolates on his hat brim.

When I was very small, Arthur would toss me into the air and catch me. Risky, yes, but thrilling.

However, he was also controlling. He preferred that my mother never wear green. He wanted me to grow my hair and keep it long, which I did. He insisted, even when my sister and I became adults, that we always celebrate Christmas together, as a family, in his home. These rules, and others, small but not to be overlooked, were obeyed. The alternative was silent fury, an exclusion from the sunshine of his personality. My sister tried to buck the Christmas trend when she had children of her own, but was intimidated back into compliance.

Else fed us, bathed us, brushed our hair and washed our clothes. (And several afternoons a week she also helped in the shop. Her roles included clerical and secretarial assistance. Arthur's grasp of English syntax was weak, at best, and his handwriting semi-legible.) She was a proud and conscientious mother, but not a tactile one – a hug, a touch were the most we would receive from her. Her relaxed physical posture, when sitting on the sofa at the end of the day, was a clench, legs and arms tightly crossed. On bad days, like Mondays (washing days, involving a good deal of physical exertion and, at least in the early years, boiling water and mangles), we learned to stay out of her path for fear of an outburst of fury. Her temper, when she felt overloaded, could be short. A slap to the leg or the head was not out of the question.

Arthur was a hugger. He liked to sit close. He never hit me, but he did spank my sister once, for some domestic infraction. My mother told her that there would be a smack when her father came home. Both Madeleine and Arthur were tortured by the expectation and the delay, and after he had administered the punishment he told Else he would never do it again.

By the fifties, he had made some progress ascending the social ladder down which he and my mother had slid thanks to the systematic dehumanization of the Third Reich and the subsequent years of wartime privation. They had arrived with nothing. Now they had a house, and of course a car, too. What followed, year by year, was a tireless, repetitive pattern of substitution and improvement, of both home and vehicle, until they reached a place of middle-class satisfaction. *Bürgerlich* once more.

Our home in Burslem – an apparently solid town, yet the buildings were seamed by coal-mining subsidence – was merely the first flag planted in the field of property ownership. We would move three more times in my first decade or so, before Arthur felt he could come to a halt. Were there echoes here of the multiple moves, made perhaps for similar reasons, of his childhood?

The first of our shifts was to a bungalow in the countryside, on a hill, next to a chicken farm. This home was freezing cold in winter, and the distance necessitated complicated school and transport arrangements for both of us girls. My mother was lonely. I was terrified of the chickens. Only my father was gratified by the choice – it fed into some fantasy or memory of rural living. Eventually our collective unhappiness persuaded him to up sticks again, back into the suburbs where there were buses, and human neighbours.

As for the cars, their exchange never stopped until his death. In the 1950s, the great British motoring marques were still flourishing – Humber, Hillman, Rover, Triumph. Every year or so, when finances permitted, there would be a switcheroo to a newer, better vehicle, although never a foreign one. As for German cars, they were deemed beyond the pale.

Not so for Richard. A black-and-white 1950s postcard from New York bears a photograph of him with his VW Beetle. 'My dears,' he writes, 'here I am with my VW, fire-engine red, black roof, all paid off in two years. Driving it gives me intense pleasure.' His need for transport arose from – and was partly funded by – a job he had accepted, teaching at the Pratt Institute in Brooklyn.

His involvement with the art college would run from 1952 to 1965, and helped bridge the financial gap created by winding down his acceptance of commercial art commissions in favour of making his own paintings. According to the Rabkins, Richard's earnings at this point went from $3,000 a month to $8,000 a year. Certainly, money was on his mind. He couldn't yet afford to turn his back on illustration commissions completely, even though time spent away from painting – which was delivering so much pleasure, he reported – was resented.

The Rabkins also observed that the move from commercial to fine art was matched by a shift in Lindner's social circle. Some older acquaintances were being discarded, to be replaced by artists like Frederick Kiesler and Isamu Noguchi.

The art department at Pratt was chaired by Fritz Eichenberg, an illustrator and wood engraver, and a fellow German Jewish refugee from Nazi Germany. Richard began as a part-time instructor in 'graphic expression', later moving on to 'design and illustration'.

Reports suggest he was a stimulating tutor and at times an unconventional one. He would buy tiny items like pins and challenge his students to draw them much larger; or to draw a nude and then, via a tracing-paper overlay, to clothe the figure. He forbade the erasing of lines: 'No eraser, ever... Every line has a reason for its existence, conscious or no.' And empty spaces in artwork were discouraged, because no place exists where a thing is empty.

New York-based artist Mary Ellis remembers being taught by Richard in the early 1960s, alongside other notable tutors like Alex Katz, Mercedes Matter and Robert Mallary. His class stood out from all the others, she says, because of its divergence from the general Pratt approach, which was to emphasize the sheer labour intensity of being an artist. Lindner's emphasis was elsewhere, stressing the importance of self-expression. He wanted his students to search for their identities and to define what it was they wanted to say. For Ellis, this was intensely enabling. He also made her feel very supported. 'He was open to anything.'

Her recollections chime with Lindner's own, characteristically contrarian views:

> I do not believe in teaching art. I think it's based more on the kind of relationship between the older artist and the young ones in a human way, rather than talking about how to paint and things like that. And I think I had a good rapport... I don't think it's important to know how to paint. It's more important to have something inside which you want to express and never mind with which medium you do this.

As a matter of fact, sometimes I did tell the students: if you cannot draw it or paint it, write it, or sing it, or, you know, just express yourself, that's the most important thing.[2]

Ellis recalls, too, Richard's own uniqueness. He was older than many of the other staff members, impressively dressed, with his ascot at his throat and his perfectly fitting outfits. She found him 'very proper', also very private. 'He had a mystique, an aura of success.'

Best of all, perhaps, he allowed his students to grade their own work.

Another student who remembered Lindner's classes sharply and fondly was Nancy Grossman, who went on from Pratt to forge a successful career in sculpture, drawing and collage. A childhood spent in upstate New York had left her desperate for a different life, an opportunity to express her inner self, and this she found at Pratt, especially in the kindred spirit of Richard.

'He saved me,' she told me in conversation. 'My own art was to look on the inside, and Richard told me: "That is exactly what is really mysterious."'

She too recalled Lindner's assignments and their emphasis on creative expression. One was all about personal dreams. He told his students to select a dream of their own from memory, write it down, then read the account aloud for their peers to evaluate. Only after that were they invited to paint their dream, and again share it for criticism. This, for Grossman, was a perfect – if daunting – example of exploring and exposing the inner self.

'He was one of us, an honest-to-goodness person, and he gave us his whole attention,' she maintained. Her friendship with Lindner continued after her course ended; it was the same with many of his students, she said. When she became an artist in her own right, Richard approved of the work so much that he introduced her to his own gallerist, by then Arne Ekstrom, who became Grossman's dealer too.

Grossman's friend at Pratt, Emanuel Schongut, was another who maintained a friendship with the artist that stretched beyond art school in the mid 1950s. Like Mary Ellis, Schongut found Lindner mysterious. 'He was the most influential teacher I had, in his own quiet way,' he told me. 'He was a small man, yet somehow larger than life. I was in awe of him, a little bit frightened, intimidated, because I admired him so.'

Schongut went on, like Lindner, to become a successful illustrator and an art teacher. 'He taught in a very quiet way, but was influential. I teach in a similar way. Instead of imposing ideas, he would bring out the student and their way of working. His key words were: "It's all about observation."'

The two were friends until the mid 1960s, when Schongut left the city. Their last meeting was in Richard's studio, where the latter was painting *Ice*, featuring a girl in goggles and striped stockings, licking an ice cream cone. 'Richard pointed to the mouth and tongue: "I enjoyed doing that," he said. "The rest was hard work."'

Intolerable though German engineering might be in my family home, a kind of schizophrenic equilibrium held sway when it came to food and culture. The language itself was forbidden in the house, although my parents found it easier and more relaxing to chat with fellow refugees in German. Being English could be a strain, an ambition never to be realized. This was underlined every time our little shop was burgled, an event that happened regularly during its lifetime. On each occasion, the local newspaper, the *Evening Sentinel*, would offer a brief write-up of the smash-and-grab, inevitably introducing my father, the proprietor, as 'foreign-born'. For all my parents' gratitude to the unpretentious Midlanders who had accepted them into their community, this was instantly identified by them as thinly veiled anti-Semitism. The public identification also exposed them uncomfortably to the light when all they sought was anonymity.

Their struggles with identity existed in the present tense, were part of the daily warp and weft. Among my parents' modest collection of books was a volume of cartoons by Osbert Lancaster, a well-born English humorist whose illustrations simultaneously mocked and upheld upper-class mores. These were appreciated in the same mental breath as *How to Be an Alien* by George Mikes, a post-war bestseller written by a Hungarian émigré turned British citizen. Famously, it covered topics like tea, queuing, cleverness (deemed bad manners by the English) and sex. This gentle mockery of their new countrymen and -women served to soften my parents' unfamiliarity and unbelonging.

(Hidden in this small library were some other, darker volumes – books about the Holocaust that came with sections devoted to black-and-white illustrations of concentration camps and their victims. These books didn't introduce me to the knowledge of my family's history. Those facts arrived so early in my consciousness that it seems as if I always knew, never needed to be told. Instead, they belonged to a larger ritual: the obligation to acknowledge any and all public considerations of the recent past. It included watching every television documentary about the Holocaust – and there were many as I grew up – in pin-drop silence. Nothing was ever discussed, yet revisiting the charnel-house imagery in whatever form seemed to serve as witness being borne.)

My own personal appetite for books had started early – somewhere between the ages of two and three, according to family legend – and while I was making my way through English children's classics, and whatever else I could lay my hands on, I was also fed German equivalents, in particular *Struwwelpeter*, the visionary volume of cautionary tales by Heinrich Hoffmann, which planted seeds of Teutonic cruelty into my nightmares.

(The other nightmare figure of my childhood was contributed by Richard. It was that watercolour of the two capering clowns entitled *Grock & Fratellini*, which for a while hung on my bedroom wall. The left-hand figure, with tufty hair and a painted face not so very different from the demon in Stephen King's *It*, terrified me just a little more than his possibly voodoo-inspired brother, with the blue jacket, top hat and yellow gloves. Both would shift and dance menacingly when I was feverish.)

Struwwelpeter, meanwhile, is a monster of self-neglect, a child with a mane of hair and foot-long fingernails. In Hoffmann's near-clichéd world of strict Germanic cause and effect, the children's rejection of bourgeois grooming and behavioural norms comes with terrible consequences. Little Suck-a-Thumb, for example, ends up with his thumbs cut off by 'the great, long, red-legged scissor-man'. As for Augustus, who refuses his soup for several days running, he simply turns into a matchstick. 'And on the fifth day he was dead.'

I was not a disobedient child.

Although my parents were both naturalized as British citizens in 1947, we kept a continental kitchen, to the extent that this was possible in Stoke-on-Trent, a city not exactly overflowing with delicatessens and speciality-food suppliers. Somehow my parents truffled out little local backstreet shops, usually run by Polish people, where they could buy approximations of the cured meats, sausages and breads they craved.

My mother's culinary repertoire was derived from memories of her own mother's kitchen. Chicken soup with dumplings was boiled up freshly every weekend, to meet my father's expectation. He was a soup, meat and carbs kind of guy. Midweek dinners might include *Eintopf* (a lamb stew), or *Rouladen* (cabbage rolls stuffed with beef), or *Schnitzel*, always accompanied by potatoes or noodles or *Spätzle*. And, despite a limited budget, desserts appeared often, like *Kaiserschmarren* (a kind of fried, chopped pancake, with raisins) or *Arme Ritter* (translation: 'poor knights'), which were made by dunking stale teacakes in milk and then frying them, before serving with cinnamon and sugar. There was a lot of frying.

My mother also baked cakes every week, usually following recipes in *Dr Oetker's Backen Macht Freude* – marble cake, streusel cake, plum cake in the autumn. These were served with a pot of strong black coffee at about 9 p.m., for the adults, not the children. My parents slept soundly in spite of the late slug of caffeine.

Possibly one of these cakes made its way to Manhattan, since another of Richard's postcards – this one featuring a fluffy tabby kitten with a sketch of Richard, pipe in mouth, at its shoulder – gives thanks for the 'fabulous' cake. 'It lasted me one whole day, and then it was gone. I wish I could paint as well as you bake.'

There was carp on Christmas Eve, and goose – with different dumplings – on the day itself. Lips would be curled at the thought of turkey or Christmas pudding. English food and drink were deemed lesser. For this, at least, we were happy not to be part of the group.

All of this domesticity and more was faithfully recorded by my father via cine-camera. Footage exists of both my sister and myself in the hours after our births. The black-and-white reels span Christmases, birthday parties, weekend trips and simple family scenes. The rooms of our homes seem tiny, but our mother fusses over or smiles with satisfaction at us little ones. We generally sport bows in our hair and hand-knitted cardigans over full-skirted, smocked frocks. When he appears, my father, a lifelong cigarette smoker, has a near-permanent fag end in the corner of his mouth. He wears ill-fitting sports coats and National Health spectacles, and has the wild hair of Professor Branestawm as illustrated by Heath Robinson. He looks foreign. We all do.

★

These were the Harold Macmillan years, the years of 'never had it so good'. 'Go around the country, go to the industrial towns, go to the farms and you will see a state of prosperity such as we have never had in my lifetime – nor indeed in the history of this country,' the British prime minister intoned in 1957. And in America, President Eisenhower was expressing parallel sentiments that same year: 'All countries today stand on the threshold of a more widely shared prosperity.' In fact, while the post-war mood was predictably upbeat, one nation's arc was tilting downwards, in a late phase of colonial decline, while the other country was stepping fully into its own moment as the most powerful nation on earth. Nevertheless, in this era of growing prosperity and consumerism, both Lindner brothers were finding their feet.

Richard's absorption into the culture of the United States seems to have been swifter and less of a source of discomfort than my parents' dealings with Britishness. New York, after all, is a city of many tribes, and Richard quickly rejoined his. His inner circle was a fantastic resource for the sharing of experience, opinion, meals, work, gossip, holiday homes and more. It must also have offered a buffer against a sense of exclusion, while serving as a generous mutual support system. A glimpse into the 1953 diary of Stefi Kiesler, wife of the artist Frederick Kiesler – who apparently 'greatly disliked [Lindner] until a short while ago' – suggests the depth, frequency and contents of the social interaction. There were parties, dinners, discussions of new art made, or lovers or partners. The group kept late hours, ate at favourite restaurants like Pappas and the Alpine Rotisserie, and also kept continental ways – coffee and cake at late hours.

When it came to food, Richard shared much of Arthur's taste. He too loved sludgy soups, and also never overcame that lifelong preference for the cuisine of his childhood. Evelyn Hofer often cooked German meals for him. In later years, when he became famous, Richard was invited to contribute a recipe to *The Museum of Modern Art Artists' Cookbook*, which pulled together thirty contemporary painters and sculptors, their observations on food, and some 155 recipes. He confessed to a raging sweet tooth and submitted a recipe for spice cakes.

But the sugar rush would inevitably lead to regrets, he said, and soup was his favourite food. 'I like oxtail soup and lentil soup with sausage, and I like it thick.' He remarks that he didn't have such a problem with the food he was given as an internee during World War II – indeed, he relished some of the poorer things in life. 'I love German peasant food, boiled potatoes with butter, home fries, goulash, *Weisswurst* with sauerkraut.' Here at least the brothers thought as one.[3]

By 1954, Richard was ready to take his evolution one step further and show his work. Saul Steinberg's partner Hedda Sterne introduced him to art dealer and collector (also painter and sculptor) Betty Parsons, who was once referred to as 'the den mother of Abstract Expressionism'.[4] Parsons, who had opened her eponymous gallery in 1946, represented a dazzling roster of American artists, including Jackson Pollock, Mark Rothko, Agnes Martin, Ellsworth Kelly, Jasper Johns and Robert Rauschenberg. She also represented Steinberg and Sterne.

Lindner had been working relentlessly, sometimes distracted by paid commissions, sometimes free to give painting his all when there was nothing else on the financial horizon. The deaths of Joseph Bornstein and, shortly afterwards, Jacqueline/Elsbeth interrupted this creative surge, while also possibly influencing it. After such seismic losses, he needed to escape, and went to Europe for eighteen days with Evelyn, moving from Switzerland to Italy and then Paris.

Sometime afterwards Richard started work on his biggest and most ambitious work to date, *Entr'Acte*, later known as *The Meeting*. Bringing together figures from his past and his present, it offers multiple levels of interpretation, including perhaps a statement of life affirmation, in enduring contrast to Jacqueline/Elsbeth's rejection of it.

The characters in the painting are an amalgam of the historical and the contemporary, members of Lindner's original family and his current circle, including Saul Steinberg, his wife Hedda and Evelyn. Richard's relationship with each of the three was exceptionally close.

> Within minutes at their first meeting, they both [Saul and Hedda] knew that Lindner would become their lifelong friend, and he did. Like them, he was a refugee who embraced all things American from the moment he arrived in 1941. They were all approximately the same age and had many things in common, from their personal backgrounds to their political underpinnings... They and Lindner shared the same idiosyncratic but insightful responses to much of contemporary American art and artists. Steinberg credited Lindner with a 'proto-pop [art] color sense,' one that he

shared. They had many friends in common, both abroad and in New York, which further deepened their bond. Saul was a dedicated poker player and spent many pleasant evenings playing at Sasha Schneider's apartment with Lindner and Gjon Mili. Lindner introduced them to the set designer René Bouché, and Saul and Hedda befriended him as well.[5]

Richard's friendship would also be flexible enough to span the intense, problematic relationship between Steinberg and Sterne. '[He] went to the Metropolitan Opera with Hedda and to the movies with Saul.'[6] He also babysat their cat, observing their routine. Steinberg's habit was to put a bib (a paper napkin with a hole cut in) around the cat's head prior to feeding and Richard would happily do the same.

Evelyn Hofer's photography had a role in *The Meeting*, her individual photos of Steinberg and Sterne serving as substitutes for posed sittings.

More generally, and throughout the years of their friendship, her pictures of Richard became the accepted photographic record of the man, in particular the professional man. The artist, seen in his studio against a background of his work, is charted from the 1950s to the 1970s, the paintings developing, the man ageing.

Hofer's earliest photos of Richard capture him at a remove, walking the mid-century streets of New York. But over time the focus draws closer and Richard becomes the central, exclusive figure. He is seen at the Pratt Institute, the new professor leaning on a stone balustrade or an ornate light fitting, still in the middle distance. But then the head-and-shoulders, studio (*his* studio) portraits begin, the earliest of them showing Lindner with sleeves rolled up, sitting amidst paints, palettes and brushes.

There's a comic shot, with a bowler hat and a cane, but mainly these photographs settle into a routine of the man and his canvases, the eyes becoming more tired, the expression less inviting. Succeeding as an artist seems to have exacted a price, or else imported seriousness to the small, compact figure in the simple but stylish clothes, in the sparsely furnished rooms.

For *The Meeting*, Evelyn's photos show Sterne and Steinberg, separately, seated in a garden, the husband in profile, wearing a straw hat and a white shirt, the wife in a gown and criss-cross open-toed shoes. Hedda's pose is regal, her beauty and poise unmistakable.

In Richard's painting, Hedda's gown is red and her hair auburn. She is positioned above her husband, who is now wearing a green bomber jacket with red collar and cuffs. His gaze remains blank while hers is supremely composed. While the couple dominate the right side of the painting, Evelyn fills the bottom left-hand corner, looking out but avoiding the viewer's eye. She wears a hat and gloves, in a duller shade of red, and a prosaic sweater and coat, the embodiment of frumpy.

Other seated figures around the edges include the mad king, Ludwig of Bavaria, and young but voluptuous Lizzy Lindner, as previously mentioned. Richard in his sailor suit, with *Tante* Else, stands at the back. An enormous cat (apparently Florian, Steinberg's pet) and a corseted woman, whose undergarment itself mimics a cat's face, are positioned at the front. A wall and a door at the rear suggest a room, yet the figures do not conform to laws of scale or gravity. Some hover in the air, even as they are seated in their chairs. The space is squashed, the figures pushed together.

A tour de force of symbolic group portraiture, this complex figure painting represents both a psychological family portrait and a metaphorical interlude between the painter's past and his new life in New York. In 1962, Lindner would describe it as 'somehow significant for me as a kind of breakthrough of my European past.'[7]

Others agreed, among them the artist Robert Indiana.

What with Mad King Ludwig himself sitting there in the middle of his most famous canvas – confronting Mr Steinberg across a lady not exactly corseted in the most cuddly American bra – I suppose I did think of Lindner as a bridge between European Expression and a very sophisticated American Social Comment.[8]

In this one landmark work Richard had achieved an extraordinary synthesis of themes, iconic figures, cultural components, personal obsessions and stylistic development. While many of these would be revisited individually, future major paintings would break different, less intimate ground.

The Meeting was one of the eighteen paintings exhibited by Betty Parsons in Lindner's first show, which opened on 25 January 1954 and continued for three weeks. It was reviewed in the *New York Herald Tribune*:

At the Betty Parsons Gallery I found impressive paintings by a newcomer called Richard Lindner. These are representational, although the figures are swollen in size and sometimes fairly static. The pictures are still extraordinarily imaginative. There is a great air of mystery here. Complex but always disciplined design, luminous color, superb drawing mark Lindner's distinguished and completely personal expression. Best in the show are 'Clown,' 'Child's Dream,' and 'Paul Verlaine.'[9]

Another review, this one unattributed, comments:

The most downright sinister paintings of the new year so far are those by Richard Lindner at Betty Parsons. With their clear colour and pneumatic figures they are clearly indebted to Léger. But no one will think of style when faced by a single canvas which portrays, in a claustrophobic room, a sailor, a 1910 lady, a well-known New York artist and his wife, a huge Cheshire cat, a small giantess clapping her hands to her ears, the mad King Ludwig of Bavaria and a girl totally naked except for a tin hat, an iron maiden corset and black silk stockings. Such stuff as nightmares are made on. The disturbing symbolism, painted with an almost naturalism, is probably best left to an analyst, but it is clear that Lindner is obsessed by the kind of creepiness that is magnified by ambiguity.[10]

Betty Parsons's archive at the Smithsonian Archives of American Art in Washington DC lists the eighteen paintings (and one loan – *Lady and the Lion* by Hedda Sterne) exhibited, and their prices. They range from $750 for quite a few, to $1,200 for *The Child's Dream* – marked 'sold' – to $1,500 for *The Visitor* and $3,000 for *Entr'Acte/The Meeting*. As Robert Indiana observed, this painting remains Lindner's best-known work. Anonymously donated to New York's MoMA, it appeared in their display 'Recent Acquisitions 1962'. Nowadays it seems not to be on view.

Many of the works in the first show had European titles: *March militaire*, *L'Académie française*, *Wunderkind*, *L'académicien*. By the time of Lindner's second show at the Parsons Gallery, in 1956 – containing only ten paintings, but also five drawings – the titles were simpler and, with the exception of *Grand Guignol*, briefer and English: *Profile*, *Doll*, *Couple*, *Boy*. Opinion, however, seemed to be that his relationship with the Parsons Gallery was not working. Hedda Sterne observed that he was treated like a second-class citizen there. Others noted that he had a hard time financially, and was quite bitter about it. It would not be until Lindner switched galleries, to Cordier & Ekstrom, that his financial fortunes would begin to turn.

In spite of this, word about Lindner was spreading. A letter from the College of Fine and Applied Arts at the University of Illinois dated November 1956 reports that one of his paintings will appear in the 1957 'Exhibition of Contemporary Painting and Sculpture' there. The letter also asks for biographical details, which had been requested before and not supplied, implying that this might have been the second work of his they had shown.

Another approach, from William Copley of the William and Noma Copley Foundation in Chicago, dated November 1957, also complains about a lack of response from the artist. Nevertheless, it bears the good tidings that the foundation is planning to award him a grant this year. Without biographical details, however, they would be unable to deliver the award.

The last show that decade came in 1959 and included some twelve paintings. My parents were sent a preview invitation. Inside is a handwritten note from the artist, expressing thanks for yet another fabulous sweater (the third?), but apologizing for his inability to send anything himself, owing to being 'a bit broke. Otherwise all is going well.' Parsons records the sale of two of the twelve, *Homage to Nuremberg* and *The Mirror*, for $800 and $1,500, respectively. *Entr'Acte* appears again, now with a price of $1,500.

This show was reviewed, somewhat sceptically, by Stuart Preston in the *New York Times*.

> Richard Lindner's tongue-in-cheek paintings at the Betty Parsons Gallery introduce a far more perplexing and sophis-ticated variety of strangeness... Here we have 'problem' pictures in the best modern manner, impenetrable to common sense, but fascinating in their way. But, somehow, they disarmingly suggest that they are sphinxes without secrets.[11]

Another review, again unattributed, says Lindner 'cuts his figures up into pieces, laces parts of them into tight corsets, outlines other parts in black line no less confining. It's all very Freudian – I think. But whatever the meaning of all this, it is, within its postery jig-saw-puzzle limits, technically interesting.'[12]

His less than satisfactory relationship with Betty Parsons was coming to a conclusion. As Lee Hall comments in his biography of her:

> Originality, not beauty, was the quality Betty sought in her artists... Lindner combined brightly colored stylized images of decadence with features from Surrealism, from Cubism and from Expressionism. Most visitors to the gallery regarded Lindner as a Germanic aberration in the art world, as a highly skilled artist exorcising the horrors of war lingering in his own psyche. Betty thought otherwise. 'He was,' she said, 'an original. People said he was like George Grosz but he wasn't. Later they said he was the first Pop artist. He wasn't that either but that helped sell his paintings later. When I showed him, I couldn't do anything at all for him. Nobody understood his work and everybody hated what it was about. Later, when everybody got interested in Pop art, they thought Lindner was a Pop artist and then he sold very well and got a lot of attention. But he was no longer with me then.'[13]

As the decade closed, more sales were recorded, but Richard felt broke and undervalued. Predictably, he had no time or respect for the critics, who were praising him, questioning him, psychoanalysing him. Perhaps he drew some satisfaction from the fact that they were not ignoring him. His work was being shown in group exhibitions – in Chicago, in Lynchburg, at New York's Whitney Annual in 1959. He was in some transitional place, still en route.

Time had never been his friend. Being a German Jewish child of the twentieth century would condemn him to a disrupted existence and the obligation to start all over again. He called it 'the unfortunate generation'.[14] As an artist, he would complain that he was too young to join the key art movements of his era – Dadaism, Neue Sachlichkeit. What he didn't know was that time was about to offer him a helping hand. Pop was coming. Ever the outsider, Lindner would never see himself as part of that movement either, but when it embraced him and pushed him forward, he didn't say no.

9

The 1960s

I AM nine as the decade opens, twelve on the Friday night in November 1963 when JFK is assassinated.

The news arrived while I was at my Girl Guides meeting. We children, bewildered by the sudden grave expressions of Brown Owl and the other adults present, were unsettled rather than upset. Something seismic had taken place, but it was only one man's death and the fear and tragedy we saw on the grown-ups' faces didn't seem commensurate.

The Beatles entered my eleven-year-old consciousness with 'Love Me Do', their first hit. I was a pre-teen, chubby and barrel-chested. Not menstruating, not especially interested in boys. What I remember most clearly is succumbing to German measles as their debut single played.

I wasn't exactly a sixties child, being just a few years too young to be at the forefront of political change, flower power and drug taking. But it was my formative decade nonetheless. Where my sister, born in the late 1940s, had been rule-bound, held by the limited elasticity of her suspenders and roll-on corset, I was (relatively) free. My simple shift dresses, tights and hair that didn't require curlers were all symbols of comparative relaxation, to match my parents' somewhat more permissive attitude to a second child.

Academically speaking, I didn't find school particularly difficult. I enjoyed the work and felt motivated, by the flattery of success and the wish to please my parents, to apply myself. Friendship, however, was a different matter – an area where I felt unconfident, out of step. In earlier years, there had been some uncomplicated relationships with peers, but at grammar school it took me a while to settle. One ostensible best friend rejected me for another girl. On a next attempt, the friendship faltered, founded on a wish rather than a bond. I felt confused about the obligation – pushed hard by my mother – to make connections. While needing me within reach at all times, she also wanted me to conform to her sense of normality – in other words, to be socially active. She had been a 'joiner' in her youth, active in a sports club, a competitive sprinter. I would be none of these.

But then the sixties gathered pace. I lost some weight, and I found an important friend, a wickedly carefree girl named Judy, who compensated for her own rackety home life by taking risks – sexually; with alcohol; at school, by gluing a teacher to her chair. She was a social magnet. Before she was expelled, and before she and her parents moved away, she was just the friend I needed, pulling me off the good-girl path, making me laugh, teaching me to push (just slightly) against rules and enter the sexual domain.

I found myself in a 'gang' – a mixed group of teens from my own all-girls school and the all-boys one across the way. Some of those boys formed a band and, for a while, we females took up the expected role of groupies. A couple of the boys came from wealthier families and one had access to a car. Perhaps the crowning moment of my sense of the sixties – free, sexy, uncomplicated, full of possibility – was the day we all drove to a beach in Wales, listening to Lennon and McCartney's 'Good Day Sunshine': 'I feel good, in a special way / I'm in love and it's a sunny day.'

If my teenage years came with a soundtrack, they were dressed in the fashion and visual style of the era. Carnaby Street and

Kensington – home of the Biba and Bus Stop boutiques, the very epicentre of taste – were hundreds of miles away, but magazines like *Nova* and *Honey*, and Biba's short-lived mail-order catalogue, brought dispatches from the front. There was a *Honey* boutique in a local department store, where I was permitted to buy one Mary Quant minidress: pillar-box red, piped with navy blue, with patch pockets on my backside. I thought it was the bee's knees.

Other fashion glories would include an ill-fitting pair of Anello & Davide T-strap shoes, some daisy earrings, a pink-flowered miniskirt and one or two Biba T-shirts, with square necklines and full bell sleeves, in shades of plum and bottle green.

And hats. A corduroy cap, and some floppy, wide-brimmed straw jobs, two of them, sent by Richard in response to a plea from me to seek out a boutique in New York I'd read about, called Elephants are Contagious.

It surprised and charmed me that my faraway uncle, older than my own father and a stranger, would be game for a trip to an obscure clothing shop at the behest of his teenage niece. It never occurred to me that fashion might be the perfect way to connect with him, a man for whom clothes – both the wearing of them and the painting of them – was a serious business.

Something of a style icon himself, Richard was more than happy to mail me not just headgear but fashion jewellery too. Four silver Indian bangles hung with tiny bells followed, then a Native American beadwork necklace, and best of all a silver and turquoise cuff. It was stolen from me, at university, along with an antique wristwatch and a gold necklace dotted with pearls and a ruby, my birthstone, gifts from my father. Ours, it seemed, was not a family for mementoes.

And so the sixties were upon us all, a shift of cultural gears which would permeate everything – not just music and style but politics, language, class, comedy – and redefine a generation.

To be young and attuned, to whatever degree, and even in a social backwater, was to feel empowered in ways our parents and predecessors could surely only envy.

At university, in 1969, studying English, I was offered a course option called Contemporary Cultural Studies, which had been born in 1964 and developed through a synthesis of left-wing politics, feminism, sociology, post-structuralism and media studies. It was unique and of its time. To us, the students, it felt like a cutting-edge fusion, as the times and the means of decoding them became one.

Art too had joined the cultural-studies party. Mashing up cartoons, popular culture, ideas of consumerism and identity, high and low aesthetics, Pop Art, born in the fifties but reaching fruition in the sixties, was questioning received opinions and traditions. English artist Richard Hamilton, in a letter to friends, listed its characteristics as follows:

Popular (designed for a mass audience)
Transient (short-term solution)
Expendable (easily forgotten)
Low cost
Mass produced
Young (aimed at youth)
Witty
Sexy
Gimmicky
Glamorous
Big business.[1]

Did any of this apply to the *oeuvre* of Richard Lindner, an artist whose work expressed a 'melancholy engagement with the Now'?[2] The painter himself didn't think so, and few of the above terms were applicable to his work. Sexy, or sexual, perhaps. Nevertheless, something about the colours and the female forms, the popular-culture references and the hard-edged representation translated into the new. Whether for these reasons, or the 'street' references of his latest paintings, his change of representation or the closing of the gap between content and interpretation, Richard started to receive the success, attention and sales he had long desired. 'In the fifties he was a complete outsider in terms of all the conventions of contemporary art. Lindner became an artist intentionally and as a latecomer. And indeed, when he started to paint, all his friends and acquaintances were quite taken aback.'³ But thanks to the sixties he would come in from the cold, and probably his friends and acquaintances rejoiced.

After Betty Parsons felt she 'couldn't do anything' for Richard, despite having promoted his work on several occasions through the 1950s, it was time for a change of gallery. In 1959, a Swedish-born immigrant, Arne Ekstrom, had opened a space with Parisian gallery owner Daniel Cordier on Madison Avenue. Ekstrom represented Marcel Duchamp, Man Ray and Isamu Noguchi, and in 1961 he paid a visit to Lindner's studio, in the brownstone apartment where he was living on East 95th Street. The paintings, Ekstrom later remembered, 'were in the hallway, the door was unlocked, and you could have taken them – no one cared'. Ekstrom, however, decided to care. He took Richard on and a friendship was formed.

That same year the Cordier and Warren Gallery – later Cordier & Ekstrom – in New York presented a solo Lindner retrospective: 'Richard Lindner: Ten Years'. The artist was thrilled, and communicated as much to Evelyn, reporting that he had gone to 'elegant' Cordier. The show would be 'a big exhibition, all my pictures... It's fantastic.' He was also delighted to report that the gallery owners were very rich and, unlike at Parsons, he didn't have to pay for anything – frames, catalogues, nothing.

This was useful. Richard's fortunes were not transformed overnight. A member of his circle reported that the gallery went on to provide him with a stipend in exchange for his work. For the financially stretched artist, this would have been welcome in the short term. Later, however, when the paintings appreciated in value and sold well, he would not reap the benefit.

Meanwhile, a *New York Times* review found the 1961 show 'shot through with irony and a kind of wild, bitter humor... Lindner shows no mercy to his subjects and attacks the shams of everyday life with the poetic precision of a surrealist as demolition expert.'[4] This may have delighted the artist too.

Also in 1961, Sidney Tillim published a monograph about Richard under the aegis of the William and Noma Copley Foundation. Esoteric in tone, Tillim's paper sought to position the artist in history, geography and society:

> Lindner's is a German art that has only gradually been Americanized and 'modernized' by the taint of authority and the rebellious and lascivious subjectivity of his images... His imagery reflects almost a crush on America's brassiness and its kitsch... Lindner remains both fascinated and repelled by bourgeois intimacy.[5]

Like Werner Spies – who observed, 'Lindner became a painter by virtue of distance, the distance of the émigré. Without New York, as he put it, he would never have started to paint at all'[6] – Tillim asserts:

> Lindner's German experience did not begin to become intelligible to him until after his arrival in the United States... specifically not until painting became an instrument of reconciliation with a life of continuous change...
>
> On his very first day in New York, Lindner recalls, he saw a boy of about twelve, completely drunk. And on his

first visit to Harlem he saw a Negro dressed entirely in leopard skin – suit, hat, shoes. This, he insists, could never have happened in Germany. Thus he finds New York 'unreal' yet somehow familiar. It is, he says, the only place in which he never felt that he was a stranger.[7]

So the perpetual outsider, the tourist, the observer, had found a home, in a city that was itself a kind of muse. Moreover, Tillim's interest in Lindner was going to have a role in the chain of events that would lead to the *Sergeant Pepper* cover and a shift from obscurity to a kind of ubiquity, for a time. Tillim, an artist himself, with an interest in figurative as well as abstract art, and a taste for popular culture, was commissioned to write another appreciation of Lindner, this time to accompany a collection of photographs of Richard and his studio, taken by Evelyn Hofer, all to appear in 1962 in the French magazine *Aujourd'hui*.

This was the article that caught Jann Haworth's and then Peter Blake's eye. Its opening page – a shot of five shelves in Richard's home loaded with masks and toys, games and curios – is an unwitting harbinger of the collages that returned to fashion in the 1960s and became so redolent of the era. To my great surprise, my parents even permitted me to assemble one on the walls of my bedroom, a mess of cut-out images and *objets* glued to the wallpaper in an ever-widening arc.

Other pictures from *Aujourd'hui* show the artist in front of his painting *The Meeting*, with works in progress on an easel and stacked against walls, and more of the brightly coloured memorabilia and found objects. Tillim's shorter essay delves into the Lindner psychology, talks of exorcism and magic, describes an odyssey – the further Lindner distances himself in order to plunge into the pathology of daily American life, the more he returns to his starting point.

Whether this analysis is correct or not, the works Richard would paint during the coming years were to become the ones most identifiably his, in style and content, and the most referentially American. *Moon Over Alabama* (1963), *The Street* (1963), *Coney Island II* (1964), *42nd Street* (1964), *Disneyland* (1965), *Ice* (1966), *Hello* (1966), *Telephone* (1966), *Rock-Rock* (1966–7), *Marilyn Was Here* (1967) – the titles alone anchor them in place and culture. But the images – of rock stars, young Amazonian females, gangster-like men, guns, animals – often held within or overlapped by symmetrical geometrical shapes, frequently set against flags, bunting, street signs or other quotidian US objects, and all in dazzling colours, revealed an artist who had hit his stride, and found a visual language that synthesized a life, an interior journey, a giant step from one epoch and continent to another.

He was moving outward, leaving behind the overtly personal references and the figures from European history, although there would be a couple more 'caricature portraits' in the early 1960s, one of *Louis II* (the Bavarian Ludwig) in 1962, and *Napoleon Still Life* in 1963.

An army of women was coming, the substantial females who would tend to characterize and dominate the work – and the men – in the Lindner universe. Plenty of commentators have noted the artist's perverse interest in monumental women. The paintings obviously give rise to suggestions of voyeurism, as did Richard's taste for hanging out in department stores like Macy's to watch the female parade. 'Macy's is the greatest museum in the world,' he said. 'You can study the people, the objects, the smells. Even the chandelier department is a sort of phony Versailles.'[8]

Larry Rivers's postscript to Lindner's life includes an account of the artist tracking through a variety of stores, like Bloomingdale's and Gimbels, watching women at the underwear tables, or going into changing rooms, to emerge and pose in front of the mirror. Men, in comparison, were dull, pathetic partners, and that's how he painted them, secondary and subdued, despite their gangster garb.

Lindner's female iconography, sensational and striking, draws forth much in the way of art-critical analysis. The women are courtesans, cowing their clients; they are Lulus, challenging the bourgeoisie; they are updated versions of the pioneering woman; or robots of the streets, striding forth in their unapologetic costumes, walking embodiments of social satire. Secrecy, power, 'the mysterious relationship, the misunderstanding, the "unresolved secret between male and females which creates the erotic"', as Richard himself put it.[9] He believed that women were the more interesting sex, with their creative and crazy interior lives, their tendencies to fantasize in front of mirrors, or paint their faces.

But the question surely arises: where is the line between Richard's paintings and his personal relationships? Hedda Sterne said the women were Lindner's daydreams and his fears. Others observed that he saw women as if from a child's perspective, oversized. It's hard to divorce his own sexuality from the work – a sexuality that was the subject of sideways comment from several of his female friends, including Evelyn Hofer, Sterne and Ala Damaz.

And then there's his mother, that figure of obsessive distaste who arises repeatedly in interviews, seeming always to hang heavy, like baggage, somewhere in his consciousness. He talked, in one instance, about the mother image that, for the male, never disappeared. The domineering mother/wife. Surely she had a contribution to make, to the crucible of content which gave birth to Lindner's majestic females, with their space-filling bodies, expressionless faces, omnivorous lips and blazing eyes?

Lindner denied they were erotic figures, despite the fetishistic clothing, the underwear, the nudity. And there is little in the way of sexual gratification to be found in the paintings. These women simply, and coolly, inhabit a sexualized society, a late-capitalist world of commodification.

They wear corsets, of course, but also seamed stockings and constricting clothes with buckled collars and armour-like sleeves. *West 48th Street*, from 1964, presents the head and upper torso of a woman in a pink hat that could serve as a bucket, a breastplate of a garment and armpit-length gloves. Her pink and blue handbag sits in front of her. Riding gear is detailed in *New York City IV*, dated 1964, and in the famous *Double Portrait*, said to be of Peggy Guggenheim, from 1965, the white-haired dame wears astonishing sunglasses and a metallic hat of fearsome proportions. It's a costume parade that never ends, that magnetizes and distracts with obsessive details, exquisitely evoked, like the shimmering satin or leather coat, piped with red, in *The Street* (1963), or the skin-tight purple trousers of *Hello* (1966) and their perfect crotch-aligned seaming.

Richard was familiar, from his commercial art experience, with the drawing of women's clothes in lingering and minute detail. It was a technical strength he could bring to the accumulation of cultural, personal and social ideas given form in his painting. He had been working, honing all this, for more than a decade. It had seemed like his own, lonely vision. But not for much longer.

In 1962, as Jann Haworth reported, Lindner's art was exhibited in London, at the Robert Fraser Gallery. In a postcard to Evelyn, Richard enumerated the events now massing around his work: the London show, running from 12 June to 7 July; participation in a mixed show at New York's MoMA, supported by a full page in *Harper's* magazine; the Copley Foundation book; and the *Aujourd'hui* article. It was marvellous. But he had earned it.

Known as 'Groovy Bob', and perhaps best remembered for the paparazzi shot of him handcuffed to Mick Jagger after a drug bust, Fraser only began as a gallerist that self-same year of 1962, at the age of twenty-four. He launched his space with a controversial display of Jean Dubuffet's work, but the

Offenbach by Richard
Lindner, 1935 or '36.

One of the famed
Barnes piano
adverts, 1936.

The Meeting by Richard Lindner, 1953,
Museum of Modern Art (MoMA), New York.

Ice by Richard Lindner, 1966,
Whitney Museum of American Art, New York.

Crayon drawing by Richard Lindner for his niece Elsbeth, 1967.

Lindner show must have come soon after, among Fraser's very earliest exhibitions. Later, his Duke Street space in Mayfair would become one of the Swinging Sixties' hippest focal points, showing artists like Bridget Riley, Andy Warhol and Gilbert & George. Its 1966 Jim Dine show would lead to prosecution for indecency.

Lindner visited London for three days in 1962, for the show. He reported to Evelyn that he had sold three pictures, and also received very good reviews. Perhaps he was referring to the rather stunned comments in *The Times*:

> Not the style, which is eclectic but has a hard, flashing brilliance of colour and pattern, but the tone of Mr Richard Lindner's painting is disturbing. It revives, fresh-minted in New York, the peculiar, brutal lasciviousness of Weimar Germany... The satire – or rather the 'period' evocation of perversity and corruption – is ugly and unforgiving, but the paintings themselves, weirdly compounded of Cubist, Surrealist, Dada and Bauhaus elements, command respect. They repel and fascinate.[10]

As far as I know, the other Lindner contingent, my own, in Stoke-on-Trent, was completely in the dark about these events, both the exhibition and its artist's presence. In a postcard to his brother, dated early February 1963, Richard is still procrastinating about the idea of a visit: '1964, definitely, I hope to visit... This year I have to stay here and teach, otherwise I will lose my pension.'

The mixed show at MoMA in which Lindner was included was scheduled for 1963. It had been a tradition at the museum to present a combined exhibition every few years, displaying artists deserving of greater exposure and selected for variety, not similarity. Titled 'Americans 1963', this one would include ~een painters and sculptors, among them Robert Indiana, Claes

Oldenburg and James Rosenquist. It was to be the last of the 'Americans' exhibitions, curated by Dorothy Miller, who was dubbed a clairvoyant for her ability to select artists who would go on to prominence. Richard wrote her a gracious thank-you note for the 'magnificent exhibition'. 'It is a marvelous and significant cross section of American Art today. I feel very honoured to be included.'

That inclusion alongside younger artists identified as members of the Pop movement, and the degree of resemblance between his subject matter – and in some cases style – to theirs, created the link that would connect him to the new 'school', the one that Richard would define as the first truly American movement. Previously his reputation might have been deemed an underground one. Andy Warhol, for example, was said to have been an admirer in the 1950s. No longer merely highly respected but obscure, Lindner was beginning to receive significant recognition, both for what he was and for what he wasn't.

A review of 'Americans 1963' asserted as much:

Richard Lindner… combines Léger with Balthus, John Held Jr., a touch of Mondrian and a taint of genius. But he is a pure artist and given his assumptions (which might be from Wedekind or Rilke), he builds on them with concentrated skill… Rosenquist could learn something from the edges of a Lindner.[11]

And the following year, *Time* magazine pinpointed the

uninformed urge to link his art to the latest fads of the newest artists. But Lindner is sixty-two; his paintings are a liaison with the past and Europe. Groomed by Dada and formed by Cubism, he shows how the art that shocks today is resolutely linked to the art that shocked yesteryear.[12]

Richard himself would make it his business to deny membership in the Pop Art movement at every opportunity, and there were many. 'I am not a Pop Artist,' he told one interviewer. 'I cannot be one because I was not born in America.'[13]

Dore Ashton, who would write the introductory essay to a coffee-table book devoted to Richard, published in 1970, commented: 'Even such bona fide representatives of Pop art that admire him recognize that he is something of a strange bird in their midst.'[14]

No matter. Suddenly he was everywhere – included in a show at London's Tate Gallery in 1964, entitled 'Painting and Sculpture of a Decade, 1954–64', and the 'Second Biennial of Contemporary American Painting' at the Corcoran Gallery of Art in Washington DC. In 1965 he would participate in the exhibition 'Erotic Art 66' at the Sidney Janis Gallery in New York, and, best of all, there would be another big solo exhibition, at Galerie Claude Bernard in Paris in May.

Art Voices, in its Fall '65 issue, published a statement specially written for them by Richard, revealing 'the sources of his art':

I am fascinated with
the hidden isolation between male and female...
the false shadows of Broadway
the isolated object of a woman's knee
the immobile mobility of NY City
the Courrèges '65 look
the mortal truth of Disneyland...

He no longer needed to teach at Pratt and ended his involvement there. Instead, in 1965, he taught briefly at Yale, and also went back to Hamburg, his birth city, for a three-month guest lectureship at the Hochschule für Bildende Künste, time enough to paint *Disneyland*, a classic, in which one of his monstrous women, with riding crop and whip, a parrot's head between her legs, offers her profile against a background of US bunting, metallic wings and the scoreboard of a pinball machine.

The painting grew out of a visit to Los Angeles, where he saw the 'usherettes' at Disneyland dressed in the kind of clothes he painted – short skirts, low-cut blouses and jockey caps, with riding crops in hand. It was a perfect Lindneresque inverted world: 'The children are actually the grown-ups since they are in their domain, and the adults are really the bizarre ones, yes, it was a shock to me, one of my strongest impressions.'

Interviewed in Hamburg, he confessed to admiring the city: 'Orderly, clean, wealthy, no beggars, like in America.' (Perhaps a touch of post-Teutonic irony here?) However, unlike his working sojourns in Paris, where people he knew washed in and out, he was on his own.

> I am suffering because I know and have seen every cufflink in every store, but I don't know any people. When I walk around alone at night in the inner city, it looks at first as if great things are happening. But the fact is there is nothing going on, there is not one person around.[15]

He was sixty-four, successful and alone.

Then came the events of 1967 – the *Sergeant Pepper* album release and all the hoopla that accompanied an artistic achievement of such all-round, landmark originality. The music, of course, became legendary, mythic, but the cover art achieved its own iconic status too. And Richard's visit to the UK and his final arrival at his brother's doorstep came on the crest of a wave, which perhaps helped propel him through the stress of close encounters with family.

Returning to London on 28 December 1967, Richard also resumed the company of artists, the tribe with which he felt most at ease. Peter Blake and Jann Haworth spent several evenings with him, sometimes joined by Arne Ekstrom. Richard revealed he had two studios, one for drawing and one for painting. He also offered a snapshot of the inspirational impulse, recounting a meal with an English girl who was wearing a micro-miniskirt. He asked her why she wore it and she said, 'To say "No".' This led to the painting *No*, a seminal sixties image of a long-haired woman seated in the hoop of the letter O, against a Stars and Stripes background. Its current location is unknown.

For a change of scene, Blake and Haworth took Richard on an outing to Brighton, to visit the museum in the nearby village of Bramber. The work on display there represented Englishness at its most eccentric: small stuffed animals arranged into tableaux, playing cricket, taking tea and so on, assembled by an amateur taxidermist, Walter Potter. Richard's response, as noted by Haworth in her diary, was typical:

> He thought Potter must be an imbecile – first he said, 'Not too bright', then 'dim', then 'stupid', then 'moron', and eventually, two hours later, 'Imbecile, to carry on that stupid task for eighty years!' He said it in such a funny way. Bramber made us talk of death and a 'real age'. [Richard], like us, doesn't feel grown up yet... He said he's afraid to make a will lest he dies. I can't say how I hope he has many more healthy years.[16]

He had become famous enough to take up the role of cultural touchstone, appearing in articles beyond the fine-art pages of newspapers. An early-sixties *New York Times* piece entitled 'Artists' Row' peered into the brownstones of the artists' colony located in Manhattan's East Nineties.[17] There's a touch of Habitat to the quirky shots of 'unpretentious yet distinctive' interiors dotted with strategic bowls of fruit and pot plants. Robert Motherwell and Helen Frankenthaler's living room features a fireplace 'of their own design. The owners covered the surface with wood paneling and used a spice rack as a mantelshelf for matches and small objects. The large painting is by Rothko.' An original, not a poster.

Other sitting rooms and dining areas, belonging to different artists, are illustrated, and then we come to the library–bedroom of painter Richard Lindner. Wealth had clearly not yet infiltrated his home. His bed is a mattress on a raised wooden platform; a sculpture is set on a packing case. There are white walls and floorboards, and a single bentwood rocking chair. The article says the room is saved from starkness by the 'warm colors in the handwoven bed cover, rug and pillows'. The observation is not entirely convincing; it looks like student accommodation.

A few years later, in another *New York Times* article, this one about moderately priced solutions for home offices, it's Lindner's shelves in his bedroom–studio that are being extolled. Richard lolls against the wall alongside a storage arrangement for books, electronics and paintings. A sculpture by Nancy Grossman sits among the books. The shelving is made of steel tension poles set up under the guidance of an architect, Felix Augenfeld, another émigré, most famous for the special chair he built for Sigmund Freud, which Freud took with him to London when fleeing the Nazis.[18]

In 1968, my uncle sent me the first issue of a US magazine called *Avant Garde*, a zeitgeisty, somewhat sensational large-format publication which announced itself with the smuggery of the age: 'As most of the world's ills are traceable to old imperatives, old superstitions, and old fools, this magazine is exuberantly dedicated to the future.'[19]

The 1960s were full of such self-important assertions and launchpads. *Avant Garde* would live for a mere three years, but gave birth to a typeface of the same name. Richard's painting *Ice* – the one with the girl in goggles and rainbow stockings, licking an ice-cream cone, posed within a diamond, half-obscuring the word 'Love', while a star and a Native American face are plastered across her abdomen – graces the front cover of its debut, my copy of which is hand-inscribed for me by Richard: 'This is also a painting of mine now in the Whitney Museum, New York.' Inside, among articles on Richard Nixon and the Fugs, and drawings by Muhammad Ali, is an eight-page full-colour article entitled 'Richard Lindner: The Rubens of the Love Generation'.[20]

It draws parallels between the two artists' taste for '*zoftik*' women, their unabashed visualization of their fantasies and their late success.

> Only now, in the September of his life, has [Lindner] per-fected the high-voltage style that has made him a major force in American art. Does the Love Generation's greater permissiveness toward overt sexual – and occasionally fet-ishistic – representations in art have anything to do with Lindner's emergence? Perhaps so. As Lindner himself says, 'For me it has meant a rebirth.'

A rebirth in the September of his life. An acceptance of what-ever misfit identities were being laid on top of his long-brewed style. As successes go, it was imperfect, but perhaps they always were. He would take it.

The Lindner *Catalogue Raisonné*, published in 1999, includes a five-page list of all his exhibitions to that date, three columns per page. The 1950s' shows occupy less than a single column. Those from the 1960s run to almost two pages. There was no denying the fact that he had made it. His paintings were desirable and increasingly expensive; as he told the Hamburg interviewer, everything from the Paris 1965 show had sold.

He had become a recognized and regarded figure on the world stage, a painter of renown. He was far from a young man, but still very fit, according to Hedda Sterne, slender and with good coordination. His energy levels were high. He was painting, busy. Yet there was a space in his life. And then he met Denise Kopelman.

Richard's second marriage took place in July 1969. He was sixty-eight, his new, French bride forty years younger. She had been married before, to another painter. Tall and beautiful, Jewish, an artist, Denise was the subject of much controversy among Lindner's long-standing circle of friends. Arne Ekstrom was one of the many who thought the May/September relationship ridiculous and a mistake. Ekstrom blamed Denise for coming between him and Lindner, and bringing about the end of both their professional and personal relationships.

Maria Eisner/Lehfeldt, on the other hand, warmed to Denise and became a close friend to both her and her sister, Anouk Papadiamandis. Lehfeldt is said never to have forgiven Evelyn Hofer for spreading unkind rumours about Denise.

Others commented that the new wife's influence on Richard drove him towards uncharacteristic extravagance, in the form of fur coats and a Bentley.

Richard had had a reputation for enjoying the company of beautiful women, also of affairs with younger females. Denise would seem, therefore, to have fitted the mould. Indeed, she said as much, in a conversation that took place after Richard's death: 'Richard always had girls in their 20s... Usually the relationship didn't last long, so he went on to another one. I met him at 24, so in a sense I was another one, but we married and I got older with him together.'[21]

In a letter to me dating from 1969, Richard said: 'You will know by now I got married to Denise, a beautiful French girl. It is her second marriage. She is 28 years [sic] and I am very sure you will like her. She is a very good artist and was a student at the Beaux Art in Paris.' He hoped I would meet her. I never did.

In a review of the Lindner exhibition at the University Art Gallery, UC Berkeley, that same year, there was a description not only of the art – 'sharply interesting, puzzling, mysterious. His technique is masterly' – but of the artist too:

Lindner made a novel personal appearance at the preview. He is small of figure, reasonable, articulate and apparently gentle. He is bald, with a grandfatherly outfling of unruly white hair.

No doubt his costume was his own idea – with its big-pocketed, open-collared white shirt, white trousers and shoes, leathery little black jacket, black socks, filmy white and red neckerchief and a catchall bag hung closely over a shoulder.[22]

This not entirely kind depiction of a man previously noted for his sartorial fastidiousness – accompanied by a photo of Richard, his sideburns significantly in need of a trim – comes as something of a shock. His meticulous, understated taste seems to have deserted him. Was this the 'very, very elegant man who had aged well', according to Hedda Sterne? It's hard not to conclude that marriage to a woman nearly two generations his junior might have coloured his judgement.

Predictable assumptions to one side, there is little in the way of personal comment or documents to fill out a sense of the relationship or marriage. John Githens commented that Richard was fascinated by Denise, that he loved her for her beauty.

A small number of photographs of the couple do exist. Evelyn loyally took two of them, a matched pair in which Richard is seated and Denise stands behind him. With her full fringe and long hair, she looks classically French and wholly of her era. She wears a shirt and a men's tie, paisley, with a shiny waistcoat on top. In one photo she simply looks at the camera, confident in her loveliness. In another, more comical one, she has a knife gripped between her teeth. In this one, Richard is laughing; in the other his eyes are downcast, his expression self-conscious.

In another, colour image by a different photographer, Richard is sitting in profile in that same bentwood rocking chair, pipe in mouth, a woollen scarf round his neck. He looks elderly, almost frail. Denise sits on the floor at his feet, slender and soulful. Appearing young enough to be his granddaughter, she looks their age gap and all its attendant assumptions straight in the eye.

10

The 1970s

'**B**Y the mid-'60s, at an auction at Parke-Bernet, a work of [Lindner's] goes for $20,000. It's obvious success lies at [his] feet. [He] tells Niki de St. Phalle, "It's too late. I'm too old; I will still continue to eat sliced tomatoes." But a year later when [he] again sees Niki de St. Phalle [he is] married to a beautiful young French girl and [his] eyes and skin are clear and [he] is wearing a $1,000 suit.'[1]

Richard is transformed. He's half of a couple, signing letters and postcards for two. Why did he do it? Was it any kind of a love match, or a straightforward deal between beauty and success, or something in between?

And if he was spending significantly, on high-priced clothes and new apartments, was this a sign that he finally felt financially secure? He had reason to. Sales were good and prices solid. Another sale, of a pencil/watercolour work entitled *Angel in Me*, was made at Parke-Bernet in 1970 for $12,000, in an auction room packed with a 'crowd of bearded young men and mini-skirted young women'. The sum was considered a decent figure for a non-oil. In comparison, the highest price achieved by a living artist that night was $18,000, for a piece of sculptural construction by Louise Nevelson.

As I read the postcards to his brother dating from the 1970s, however, Lindner seems in some ways unchanged by the material rewards of his achievement. In one he's kvetching about the cost of moving to a new apartment, although his current one, on East 69th Street, is too small for two. 'The rents are unbelievably high – $800 to $1000 per month.' This property search is the latest excuse for not visiting. 'We'll have to stay here for the summer, because of apartment hunting.'

In fact he was travelling more – Florida, Italy, London too – partly in response to the demands of his exhibitions. But in addition, he and Denise were making frequent visits to Paris, where her family lived. By 1971 they would purchase an apartment at place de Furstenberg, and later one in rue des Saints-Pères.

So, in circular fashion, Paris once again took a major role in Richard's life. He had been a relatively happily married exile there in pre-war days, absorbing art and forging key friendships; he used the city as a temporary studio, twice, formatively, in the 1950s, as a means of fast-forwarding his creative evolution; in correspondence, he expressed typically conflicting views of the place, finding it both hateful and beautiful. Now, in his late years, he would divide his life between the French capital and New York. In one he could be European, in the other he could return to his urban muse. 'Actually, all the sketches for my paintings are made in New York. All the ideas for my paintings come from what I see here. Then I go back to Paris and paint the pictures.'[2] Paris was the nineteenth century, New York the twentieth. He remained an indissoluble melding of both.

Returning to Europe part-time and sharing his life and his home were both massive alterations in what had essentially been a solitary existence driven by a relentless working rhythm. And critics detected a subtle difference in the 1970s paintings, the descent of a retrospective mood in which the Pop iconography faded out, and couples emerged, alongside old-style gangsters and clothing from the 1950s.

Lindner was asked about this in a conversation included in the catalogue accompanying an exhibition in Chicago, later in the decade: 'The new paintings... seem more lyric, more subdued, less strident than the work of the sixties and early seventies,' his interlocutor comments. The artist answers: 'They're European.'[3]

And, despite the celebrity and the sales, the work ethic continued to ride him hard, unlike his younger brother, who wrote in 1973 to say he was easing back a little. 'I can't say that about myself,' Richard answers. 'Rather the opposite, more work. But I'm glad about it, I like what I do, what my work is about.' He's healthy, he adds, although sadly not younger. 'The best you can do is laugh about it.'

Age had become something of a touchstone, hardly surprising considering he had entered his eighth decade. At least it was bringing with it some external markers of distinction. In 1972 Lindner was elected a member of the American Academy of Arts and Letters (at that point still known as the National Institute of Arts and Letters), an organization founded in 1898 which branded itself 'an honor society of the country's leading architects, artists, composers, and writers'. Richard compared it to the Académie française. Artist Philip Guston came on board that same year, as did another member of the Saul Steinberg set, sculptor Costantino Nivola. In literature, new members for 1972 included Walker Percy, John Berryman and Ezra Pound. In the photo gallery at the institute, Richard's image hangs two along from that of Kurt Vonnegut. The institution was, at the time, overwhelmingly white, male and elderly – nevertheless, the prestige was undeniable.

In fact, Lindner had been proposed in preceding years, including in 1968, when his sponsors had included Isamu Noguchi and Willem de Kooning. When the offer finally came, he accepted it 'with great pleasure' but then seemed to block every subsequent approach that was made, whether invitations to luncheons, dinners or reading of commencement tributes, requests for loans to exhibitions at the institute or entreaties to serve on the Department Committee for Art. His chorus of declines and apologies was interrupted only once with a yes – he did want to attend the ceremonial and lunch of his own inauguration, and to invite two guests. A note on his file establishes, however, that he 'was not bringing his wife'.

Another, separate note states that 'Lindner wants his rosette'. He was not going to go without his insignia.

For Richard, such recognition pointed up an attitudinal fault line. In a long, revealing interview in 1974, he acknowledged the split response of the creative when it came to an establishment gong: 'We are all of us dual personalities, we want to be avant-gardists and we also want to be *grands bourgeois*.'[4]

It was true, even for him, for whom bourgeois expectations and mannerisms had always inspired the deepest, most reflexive disgust. He was not guilty necessarily of that cliché of ageing, the rightward political drift, but on the other hand there seemed to be something to be said, increasingly, for nice homes and expensive suits, fur coats and a Bentley. He had nothing to prove, at least in terms of professional achievement. But he had been an outsider all his life and still felt himself to be a foreigner at heart. The core of the man was unchanged, but perhaps a little softening was taking place around the edges.

Meanwhile, the business of growing old appeared to be a preoccupation. He reported, in the same conversation, that he had tried on his award once, in front of a mirror, but had given himself something of a fright. 'A decoration immediately makes you look ten years older. When you are young, you don't get one, and when you are old you can't wear it because it's so aging.'[5]

Vanity aside, however, the insignia did come in useful once, in Paris, when negotiating over an apartment on quai Voltaire with an elderly couple who were happy to have photographs of Pétain – the disgraced leader of Vichy France – still on display.

Initially the couple were rude to Richard, so he remedied the situation by putting on his decoration. 'And at once everything changed – but instantly! *Maître*, you see – and all went smoothly and well thereafter… It was absolutely like night and day.'[6]

Ah, those bourgeois. In the end, he didn't want the apartment after all.

Clichés abound about older men fending off a sense of diminishing virility with fast cars and young women. For all that the Lindner brothers regarded themselves as atypical, both were displaying signs of predictability as they entered their seventies. Arthur still fancied himself as a motorist, still swapped his cars with regularity, still wanted to drive long distances and at immoderate speeds. It would take a couple of near misses at the wheel before we could finally persuade him to stop driving. In fact, he never fully accepted the shift and died some eighteen months after relinquishing his car keys.

Richard's marriage to Denise, meanwhile, came with its own provocations: lost or disapproving friends and colleagues, and the challenge of keeping up, of not appearing ridiculous, versus the pleasure and reinvigoration of her youthful beauty and companionship.

It was a struggle, a conscious one. 'I am somewhat confused altogether,' Richard said in 1974.

> I am an old man; but actually I am a young man, that's the truth, and not just a young man, in many ways I am a child… One keeps doing the same again. I always do again what I did as a small boy, make the same mistakes, it's all the same, nothing changes.[7]

Which mistakes did he mean? Creative? Personal? Had the passing of time, the building of a new existence on top of the old, taught him nothing? In a 1978 interview, he discussed how being a witness to cowardice and the grotesque, and belonging to a persecuted group, without a doubt developed his creative sense.[8] This surely was a speck of clarity. For Richard, the past was the motor, the defining, propulsive element in his *oeuvre*. His forced emigration contributed the method, the means of articulation. These elements were lived out in the silent power struggles that he never ceased to paint. Circumstance was an indissoluble part of him, like a bionic limb.

For Arthur, the past was dead. His life had not been built on excavation but reconstruction. He was not interested in looking back. The brothers' difference was captured in these polarized positions.

However, there was common ground still to be found, at least in a physical sense, in their demises: both would succumb to heart disease. A family weakness? The accumulated results of their shared, lifelong nicotine addiction (Richard's immovable pipe, Arthur's chain of cigarettes)? There is research to suggest that Holocaust survivors who experienced their trauma after the age of thirty – which Richard and Arthur did – lived longer lives, but probably not because of their suffering, more likely because of genetic predisposition. If they had been weaker, they would not have made it through at all.

Both men reached a kind of peak in 1974, the year in which Arthur had a brush with death, and Richard experienced the crowning achievement of his career – a retrospective that swept through Europe from Paris to Vienna via Rotterdam, Düsseldorf, Zurich and Nuremberg. Could thoughts of invading – or retreating – armies be far behind?

John Githens remembered attending the opening of 'Richard Lindner' at the Musée national d'art moderne in Paris, followed by a celebratory dinner at Maxim's. Richard had invited many of his friends to come and celebrate, even Evelyn – although she probably did not go. The show ran from January to March. In its catalogue, a conversation with Richard is subtitled: 'The Political–Biographical Approach of a Life in Three Worlds,

Europe, America and the No Man's Land of Emigration'. The exhibition included over seventy-six paintings and nearly fifty studies, a substantial display.

He had not stopped painting, did not feel himself to be coasting; nevertheless, at the age of seventy-three he would have been aware that the retrospective spanned his most iconic, most celebrated, possibly most enduring work. Whatever lay ahead, how heady the moment must have been: a six-city European victory lap redolent of resurgence and long scores finally settled.

It was while Richard was hitting these lifetime heights that Arthur had his close call with mortality. Not invited to Paris, unaware even of the Lindner moment, he was scheduled instead to undergo a simple operation to remove his gall bladder. But life-threatening complications ensued. Multiple efforts to restore order to his digestive system were made, unsuccessfully, and as the days passed Arthur's strength began to fail. The family was summoned to his bedside.

I was twenty-three, busy with my life in London, learning the editorial ropes at an academic publishing house in Mayfair, living in rented rooms in Clapham, on the unfashionable south side of the Thames. I was happy enough, sampling cultural life in the metropolis, trying to find my feet socially. Everything, however, was put on hold for that dash to a Stoke-on-Trent hospital.

I had never seen my father anything other than rotund and present. Perhaps instinctively, or else through his travails, he had learned to live in the moment, to relish the satisfaction of life's smallest appetites. That first, nicotine-rich, lung-expanding inhalation of the day; or a perfectly runny fried egg on buttered toast, washed down with a cup of thick black coffee – such small, regular pleasures-of-the-moment would give unfailing rise to a broad, conspiratorial grin.

But now he was cadaverous, half-conscious, the bones of his round skull prominent. Age had caught up with him, the strong, barrel-chested little man who was nearly fifty by the time I was born.

My mother's profile, at the hospital, was as grim as a cliff, but she would not be succumbing to anything other than determination – to keep the shop running, to maintain a supply of palatable, German, decidedly non-NHS food to her husband. If these twin demands would run her ragged for the foreseeable future, so be it.

We gathered in a group – my sister and her husband too – around the bed, the air filled with the scent of some bay rum cologne I had given my father which didn't entirely mask the baser odours of the place. Nothing was spoken, but I for one took silent leave of him, having been advised by the doctors that survival was by no means assured.

And yet he didn't die, not then, not for another decade and a half. Nothing miraculous happened, just a tough old soul refusing to give in. Like his wife, he wasn't ready to stop.

Nevertheless, for those touch-and-go days, all hands were summoned, and someone – my mother, I assume – must have reached out to Richard. As mentioned, he chose not to interrupt his European commitments to see his brother one more time. He did, however, use his influence to ensure Arthur's medical care was of the best. Summoning an American specialist in gastroenterology, he set up contact with my father's doctor at the Staffordshire Royal Infirmary. Transatlantic medical conferences were held and progress monitored. Slowly the patient began to improve – and show signs of the return of his less temperate side, fussing about recovery and his wasted legs.

Richard, for once in his life, stepped into the role of older brother, writing cards that combined encouragement with admonishment.

My doctor is a great specialist in the USA and has consulted with yours. He knows your case exactly. You must recover and be patient. You are weak at the moment, but once you are out of bed again, you will be like you were before, even your thin legs. That's just the result of a lot of lying down.

Arthur wouldn't be like he was before, not quite. After his recovery, he appeared smaller, possibly more reconciled to relinquishing a little of his investment in physical strength. For a while he was simply, visibly glad to be alive. In the early days of his return home, one of us would sleep on a camp bed at the foot of his bed, ready in case he woke up in need of assistance. I took my turn, and remember waking one dawn to see my father already alert, and beaming with the most radiant of smiles. Life, even a weakened version of it, with feeble legs, was good.

Richard continued with his peripatetic life, and his working regime. He wrote, clearly reluctantly, to a German cousin, Alfred Bornstein (no relation to Joseph) in late December of 1974, explaining that he only corresponded nowadays in very important cases. Otherwise there would be no opportunity to work. 'It's nothing personal. Even before my success it was the same.'

Clearly there had been a before and an after. Success was a marker, the place that divided the era of sliced tomatoes from this new phase of a chauffeur (for the Bentley) on the payroll. Richard was insisting that he was the same man now, although perhaps enabled with more convincing reasons to avoid the things he found a waste of time. But was he?

The June 1976 issue of *Vogue* includes a six-page spread entitled 'Lee Radziwill: Find a New Job'. The famously stylish 'younger Bouvier', sister to Jackie Kennedy Onassis, is pictured at her home, wearing a suede safari suit, a book of swatches on her lap, playing the role of interior designer, which, after 'forays into fashion editing, TV acting, and talk shows' was her new gig – 'designing suites for the American Hotels group'. Her qualifications? 'Three enchantingly beautiful, richly comfortable establishments she'd created for herself, including the Manhattan duplex shown on the next six pages.'

The facing photo shows Radziwill in a lilac silk kaftan, breezing into a library 'converted from a foyer', where hangs a large Francis Bacon, *Man in a Cage*. 'The painting never meets you head on. I think that's important,' she observes gnomically.

Subsequent photos illustrate other, heavily designed spaces in the duplex, like the 'seductive drawing room: a serene square of peony, raspberry reds, pinks, coolly curtained in lettuce green'. It's a hotchpotch of overstuffed upholstery and swagged curtains, 'cozy Victoriana, Oriental exotica'.

> Lee loves best to lunch, even to dine in an orchid-bowered, fern-green corner of her drawing room where she's shown with artist Richard Lindner. 'We talked so much that we didn't eat very much. I always have a card table in the window here when I have three or four people.'[9]

And there sits Richard, a head shorter than his host, smiling gamely up at the animated princess, trapped as firmly in the glue of the haute bourgeoisie as a fly in amber. He wears a white polo-neck sweater and dark jacket, while mounded greenery threatens to engulf him on either side. Is this what his success has made of him, lunch fodder for socialites?

It's hard not to imagine the younger, striving Richard of Paris in the 1950s ripping such an encounter to verbal shreds. Perhaps, privately, he still did.

There was another major retrospective in 1977, this one at the Museum of Contemporary Art Chicago. The museum's website allows visitors to glimpse six black-and-white views of the show, and the hang looks impressive, the canvases majestic in size and impact.[10] There were forty-two paintings, fifty-one works on paper and two 'constructions' made of wood and glass – a sizeable presentation, even if dwarfed by the European one in 1974.

The accompanying catalogue includes a conversation between the artist and the museum's director, Stephen Prokopoff, that touches on the familiar node points of Richard's history and philosophy.[11] He admits to the personal nature of his work: 'Let us say that the paintings are unconscious autobiography.' He dwells on the children, the infant prodigies who featured heavily in the early work, and their source in Nuremberg, 'a medieval town. And a mean town.' He discusses again their physiologies: 'As babies these prodigies were very ugly. They had fat bodies and small hands and feet.' He cites Einstein, Menuhin, Isaac Stern as examples.

He touches on other familiar symbols from his work: King Ludwig, the mad king who 'had the vision to create Wagner'; Napoleon – 'in many ways a genius. He not only conquered the world militarily but intellectually.'

And he muses lengthily on the United States. 'I'm not very good on America because I'm not an American, I'm a New Yorker... New York is a home town to me, a place where you used to hang around the local drug store. And I especially remember the hot summer nights that had a special loneliness.'

Prokopoff circles back to that topic, and Richard, with his crisply dogmatic perspective, seems to welcome it, evoking the isolated subjects – especially the women – of his paintings in his answer:

New York has a loneliness which is tough. You see the old ladies drinking whiskey in Schrafft's because they are lonely, rich and lonely... Yet the beauty of New York is that you can live as you like. *People pass each other though they have the desire to connect* [my italics]. But being two is more lonely than being one, because one is boredom. This all interests me.

And me too, since it seems so redolent of my uncle's psyche, or the version of him I have assembled. The anonymity of his adopted city, the contrasting impulses to make contact and to walk on by, the conflict between boredom alone and misconnection *à deux*. These recurrent facets perhaps embody his character – sociable and separate, available and hidden, taking comfort in a perverse intellectualism that tirelessly relishes turning convention on its head.

The following year, New York welcomed him back with an exhibition of recent work at the Sidney Janis Gallery. It opened in April and Richard was there, with Denise alongside him. The critical reception was warm. A review in *Arts Magazine* spoke of the 'long-awaited' display of Lindner's new work. 'It is, as expected, more of the same compelling, satirical and marvelous painting that has made Lindner one of America's leading figurative painters for the past quarter century.'[12]

Larry Rivers saw the show and

came away convinced how good he was, and how well and how long he had stuck to his guns. Oddly, what seemed new in the work were really bits of an older naturalism of Richard's. While I could take little from his way of doing things, I was more convinced of Ezra Pound's dictum that 'art is character'.[13]

Critic John Gruen attended the opening and he too was impressed with what he saw: 'The exhibition found the artist in dazzling form, with canvas after canvas producing its familiar frisson of malevolence. Lindner's creative vigor had not diminished; indeed, it had intensified and coalesced into an ever terser and more eloquent statement of pure form and gorgeous, poisonous color.'[14]

But Gruen observed that the artist himself seemed very frail at this encounter. 'A short, small-boned man with sad, questioning, pale blue eyes, he had complained of being unable to shake a recent bout of the Russian flu, a bout that caused him to lose some 15 pounds.'[15] On Lindner's perennially slender frame, this was a significant loss.

Gruen and Lindner made arrangements for an interview destined to appear in *ARTnews* magazine, one in a series of such conversations that would eventually be gathered in a book. The list of artists would include Francis Bacon, Saul Steinberg, Agnes Martin and Jim Dine. 'We'll have an elegant lunch, and then we'll go back to my apartment and talk,' Lindner told Gruen.[16]

By the time they met, Denise had returned to France. Richard was in one of his anti-Paris phases: '[It] is *so* boring... Just to see the color of a New York truck or taxi excites me! There's life in New York; Paris is dead.' And yet New York disappointed him too.

> I mean, I've never had a bad review, but somehow I've never really had any real recognition in America. Critics and museum people just never knew what to do with me or where to place me. In Europe, my work hangs in the best museums and things are not so confusing.[17]

The two men strolled back from the restaurant to Richard's 'comfortable and immaculate' apartment, returning to the theme of alienation: 'I met all the New York artists, but I was always an outsider. I didn't fit in. You see, I wasn't part of any movement. I made a good living as an illustrator, but I got very tired of it.'[18]

As for composition:

> Subject matter for me is always a man, a woman, a child and a dog. Dogs, like children, are the real grown-ups... My paintings have a lot to do with balance and composition. I like structure. As for the women in my paintings, you have only to look at my wife to know that the women I paint are not at all my type.[19]

He expands on his Amazonian females, admitting there is 'the bordello aspect' to them, while defining them as the superior gender who have seen through men and their vanity, who have learned to enjoy sex, who have greater senses of both realism and fantasy. He defends himself against accusations of being a woman-hater, something he discussed with Bill de Kooning. 'The fact is, we love woman. I'm looking forward to the day when a woman is president. It's the most logical role for her.'[20]

Richard is at ease, treading the territory he has staked out as his own. There will be no rebuttals by or challenges from Gruen, not at this distinguished moment. Whether satisfied or not by the recognition bestowed upon him, when it comes to decoding his own creative DNA, the stage is his.

Two days later, on 16 April 1978, he was dead.

John Githens's memory of that evening is that he and his wife Ingeborg were at Evelyn Hofer's apartment, invited to eat dinner there with Richard. Denise would not be joining them. She was in France, a common occurrence, according to Githens. Others made the same observation. Her frequent, lengthy absences seemed to be a sore and suspicious subject with some of Richard's friends.

Lindner surprised the gathering by failing to arrive at the expected hour and Evelyn became concerned, eventually phoning the super at Richard's building, asking him to knock on his door.

When entrance to the apartment was gained, Richard was found lying on his bed, fully dressed but no longer alive. The comment he had made of Joseph Bornstein, who expired in his sleep, had held true for him too: 'Death was pretty good to him.'

His final resting place comes, in some ways, as a surprise. Lindner was buried on 20 April at the Westchester Hills Cemetery in Hastings-on-Hudson, a river town in Westchester County, some twenty miles north of New York City. Saul Steinberg made reference to the interment in a letter dated April 1978:

> All this dampened by the death of Richard Lindner, the old friend with whom I became closer in the last few years. He died in his sleep, age 77, without any illnesses, operations, or torments. Along with a few friends I brought him to a sad suburban cemetery. But the loss and the emotion are now slowly hitting me.[21]

Westchester Hills is a noted Jewish burial ground, known for its roll call of artists, performers and creative people. George and Ira Gershwin are buried there, as are the museum-founding Guggenheims, and acting teacher Lee Strasberg, and singers and producers – and furriers and chocolate makers. The imposing mausoleums containing the remains of the cemetery's most famous inhabitants are grouped nearer to the entrance, off a busy suburban highway. Richard's grave is a simple flat stone, to be found at the furthest, uppermost edge of the property, where it borders on green wilderness.

According to the cemetery's records, three adjacent plots were purchased at the cemetery forty-eight hours after Richard's death by his wife Denise, acting swiftly. Dealer Nancy Schwartz reports that she and Denise toured the cemetery together prior to the burial, and that the young widow was disappointed with the grave's remote location. Was she following Richard's request or instructions to bury him there? Had they discussed such an eventuality? Richard had apparently joked that he had married a young widow to take care of his estate. He had been age-conscious. The likelihood of forethought is strong.

Then again, as a fervently non-observant Jew, would Richard have chosen to be buried in a cemetery attached to a synagogue out in the suburbs, in a bucolic commuter township, removed from the city beat that had been his passion? It seems difficult to square this with his many contrarian, anti-tribal views, but according to Schwartz, Lindner was, in his own particular way, very Jewish; he had wanted for a long time to have an exhibition in Israel.

Obituaries followed. Larry Rivers observed that Richard's notice in the *New York Times* did not appear on the front page, thus establishing that he was not a 'world figure'. Nevertheless John Russell, the British-born critic who wrote it, denoted him among the foremost figure painters of the twentieth century's second half with a private mythology in contemporary art as commanding as any. The article adopts a wry tone in places, pointing out that, by Richard's own account, the decisive moment in his career, in the early 1960s, was 'when his intentions were confused with those of Pop Art, and he found himself a universal favorite for reasons that were no part of his general design'.[22]

Russell commented that Richard was never deceived by this historical accident. He did not point out that the absurdity fitted neatly into Lindner's world view that saw its operating laws as perverse, ridiculous and cruel, his own role always slightly misaligned. As he had said in 1972, 'I belong to an in-between generation... If I were to investigate myself, I would say that this man was born in between generations, between the Dadaists and a more recent generation of Americans. Perhaps there are other displaced artists like myself who form a sort of unconscious movement.'[23] Or perhaps there were none, although two decades later curator Judith Zilczer would group Lindner in a distinguished set of post-war artists including Balthus and Francis Bacon while simultaneously defining him as detached from any group or movement. His was the art of the outsider. She called it the circus of the absurd.

But Hilton Kramer's obituary pointed out that exact cosmic joke: 'It was part of the comedy of [Lindner's] career – a comedy he savored with appropriate irony – that art history, after at first shunning him for what he was, then acclaimed him for something he was not.'[24]

Kramer had published a full-colour, illustrated monograph on Richard in 1975. But now he was also writing his tribute as a friend, one who had eaten dinner with the artist only a few nights before his death. Despite looking a little tired and drawn, Richard had seemed very much himself, 'gentle, affable, amusing and wonderfully intelligent'.[25]

Kramer went on to point out Lindner's double endurance of life as a refugee, first in Paris, then in New York. This experience of the world, 'much of it painful', pervaded his art, and rendered it more personal and more European than anything he found in New York, even if the culture he found in the United States gave him a pictorial language to depict the 'merciless universe', the erotic menace and the historical subtext. 'The echoes of Weimar and the Hitler era are never insisted upon, but are always clearly there... Only in the refuge of America could [Lindner] have achieved what he did, and only in the horrible dislocation of European life could he have been formed as he was.'[26]

A memorial service was held at the Janis Gallery on 6 May, in the late afternoon, with Richard's most recent work still hanging on the walls. Richard Oldenburg (brother of Pop Art sculptor Claes), the director of MoMA, was the first to speak. Just prior to Richard's death, a rumour had been circulating that MoMA was about to award Lindner a retrospective, but this was not mentioned, nor subsequently converted into fact.

Sidney Janis was next at the podium, 'grave and at the verge of tears', according to one observer. He was followed by Saul Steinberg, whose admiration was enlarged by his personal friendship, and who described Richard as 'an aristocrat'.

Steinberg would be invited to write the commemorative tribute to Lindner for the American Academy of Arts and Letters on 15 November that same year, an occasion that would pay tribute to four other members, including designer Charles Eames. It was planned that Steinberg's eulogy would be read by Helen Frankenthaler, but after she reported that she could not attend, other artists were proposed and eventually the job was taken by the architect I. M. Pei.

Steinberg's tribute exists on file at the academy and the one read at the Janis memorial might have been identical, but there is no record of it. However, the Steinberg archive at Yale's Beinecke Library contains his notes and various drafts, all sweetly detailed with vignettes of the man whom Steinberg recalled with affection and tenderness. 'I tell these stories because I want to remember Richard as a playful and poetic man.'[27]

He recalled meeting Lindner in 1945, in a New York they had known previously from cinema and photos. He remembered that

> we were amazed by the fantastic colors of the city – the unexpected sight of the taxicabs colored in those days in the brilliant red, yellow, gold, blue and dark green of the Raffaello's Madonna dresses, the alarming sunsets, the neon lights and the many derivations of Cubism disguised as architecture, girls and neckties.
>
> [Richard] looked more like a man of the eighteenth century, elegant and light, a whispering man with a memorable profile, the amused smile of the philosopher and that rare sight: an intelligent eye.[28]

The last speaker at the memorial was Nancy Grossman, the sculptor whom Richard had taught at Pratt, and encouraged and supported afterwards. 'Richard was the first person who made me feel valid as an artist,' she told the room.

> I was sixteen years old when I met him and like many of his students was astonished and upset to find that Richard, an adult, acknowledged and valued those magical interests

which had been stifled in us from childhood... Because he was open to life and he celebrated life, he encouraged us to explore those deeper feelings within us from which art comes. He strengthened our abilities to express our personal universes.

Art was his whole life and his life was his art. There was never a person who could amuse himself better with everyday things. He saw everyday things the way that children do, as miracles... and he helped us to do the same.

She concluded by quoting Richard's own words from the catalogue to the 1963 MoMA exhibition which had cemented his celebrity:

I cannot talk about painting. I have now even doubts that there is such a thing as art in general. More and more I believe in the secret behavior of human beings... To search and to follow that inner silence is to live a life of the highest order. Is this art?[29]

With this, the formal proceedings ended, leaving the hundred or so gathered to mingle and disperse.

After the service, gallery owner Betty Parsons wrote to Denise, enclosing the words she had written about Richard and read to Saul Steinberg, who had encouraged her to forward them to Richard's widow:

He painted the hummingbird and the eagle
Inside people
With the authority of a giant.

In July of that same year, Alexandre Alexandre, one of Richard's oldest friends, from the pre-war Paris years, published a valedictory piece in *Novum*, a German graphic-design periodical. The article was written, Alexandre said, on a rustic table that had once stood in the Paris studio of Richard and Elsbeth Lindner. This and other curios had been gifted to him, he explained, in the first letter he received from the couple after the war, telling him he could have all their furniture.

Alexandre had met the Lindners in 1937, in that same small Parisian studio.

> A small, frail man, practically bald-headed, lying face-down on his couch and raising his head to look at me suspiciously. At the drawing-desk stood Elsbeth Lindner, a dark-haired, beautiful young woman. Soon we were close friends and I was probably the first to discover his talent and to foretell his great career which, however, was very long in materializing.[30]

For all his long-standing admiration, Alexandre chose to use this late opportunity to be strangely frank about the man he had known, describing his dead friend – as Evelyn Hofer did – as 'an imaginative storyteller' and letting the air out of some of Lindner's more startling reminiscences, including the encounters with Hitler in Munich, and the canard of Richard's service as a British soldier. Lindner and Alexandre had in fact been interned together at the Villemalard camp near Blois in 1939. 'After the German invasion we were set free and we, i.e. Lindner, a photographer Kirchberger, and myself, tried to make our way to Lyons – a torture for Lindner, who had never tried to hide that he was a coward and despised heroes as "unimaginative fellows".'[31] So much for those tales of arrests, handcuffs and daring escapes. This intimate account of shared wartime experiences has the ring of plausibility about it.

Alexandre also commented that it was in Lyons that Richard learned Elsbeth wanted to divorce him in order to marry Joseph Bornstein. 'For Lindner this was a heavy blow, for he regarded Elsbeth as his "property".'[32]

The Alexandre/Lindner friendship had been one of those that suffered – at least for a while – from Richard's pattern of closeness followed by withdrawal. Perhaps this accounted for the critical edge in Alexandre's elegy. A gap of some decades had opened up between the men, dating from the period of Elsbeth's suicide in 1952 until the seventies, when Richard, now famous, had chosen to call his old friend and invite him to his 'impressive retrospective' in Paris. 'It was a wonderful exhibition and our old cordial friendship seemed about to revive.' But Alexandre detected in the artist the same sense of existential anxiety that had hung about him in the pre-war years. Richard was once again sensing political concerns, 'reactionary conditions' in the air. 'But I have never known peace and in this sense I have the feeling of belonging to a lost generation,' he said.[33]

Displaced, lost, born at the wrong moment. Restless, isolated, spiritually discordant. Richard's discomfort with his place in the world seems to have infused his identity at every level – creatively, socially, psychically. Political peace and the peace of the soul were always strangers to the man, Alexandre observed. 'This unfulfilled yearning already showed in 1937/38 when I met him.'

So the sad eyes, the melancholy resting face were neither new nor the product of wartime sorrow and loss. This had been the younger, European man as well as the starting-over New Yorker. Perhaps it had been the boy as well, a stranger in his own family – critical of his mother, patronizing towards his father, largely remote towards his only surviving sibling.

Alexandre's portrait is a tragic one, dwelling presciently if romantically, at its conclusion, on the two major Lindner shows in Paris in 1977, which received muted responses. 'Was it this lack of echo on the part of the press, was it the generally diminishing interest of the public which finally broke this ever-fearful, vainly peace-seeking heart?'[34]

Alexandre's question hangs in the air still, now, some four decades later, with Lindner's reputation all but disappeared from view, his art rarely shown, his name practically unknown. If asked, what would Richard have chosen in the end – creativity or reputation? His art was his bulwark against the world. It mattered intensely to him that it was seen and understood. But if it were not, and if the reactionary conditions he had sniffed in the air had started to gather once more, would that have destroyed him? I don't believe so. The work was done, the paint applied, the integrity maintained. Nothing, not flames or dust, or even forgetting, could eliminate that.

Artists disappear from public view when no one remains to promote them, extol them, bolster their value, and Lindner is an object lesson in that slow process of decay. None of the agents, gallery owners, museum directors or contemporaries who praised and admired him during his lifetime is still available to hold up his work. And nor is his second wife.

Denise was reportedly devastated by Richard's death. She knew theirs had been an unconventional marriage, but viewed it as an extraordinarily close one, permanent and strong. She also felt that the union had been arbitrarily and tragically cut short. The same turned out to be true of her own widowhood. Denise Lindner died in a car crash in 1985, some half a dozen years after her husband. The accident took place in France, as Denise was driving herself to her apartment in Trouville. According to Nancy Schwartz, the crash had been terrible, 'unnecessary', the result not of a collision but of a burst tyre. Denise was not buried alongside her husband but in Paris, France.

During the handful of years in which she did survive him, the *Catalogue Raisonné* records, Richard's art continued to be shown internationally, but with diminishing frequency. His estate was represented by Galerie Maeght in Paris, and there was a show of his work at the Fondation Maeght, Saint-Paul-de-Vence, in 1979, and another under Maeght auspices that same year in Zurich. Individual items were also loaned to exhibitions all over the world, from Tehran to Tokyo. The Baltimore Museum of Art included him in a show called 'Master Drawings and Watercolors of the Nineteenth and Twentieth Centuries', which toured, from 1979 to 1980, the Guggenheim Museum in New York and Des Moines Art Center in Iowa, making two stops in Texas and wrapping up at the Denver Art Museum in Colorado.

Meanwhile, the American Academy of Arts and Letters had wanted to put together a show to commemorate four recently deceased members of its department of art: Naum Gabo, William Gropper, Richard Lindner and Abraham Rattner. But the institution was unable to obtain work from the Lindner estate. It tried approaching the Galerie Maeght, to be told that Mrs Lindner agreed to lend from her private collection and should be contacted directly. But a letter to Denise went unanswered.

In England, no one had bothered to reach out to the other branch of the Lindners. The first we heard of Richard's death was an obituary in a British newspaper.

Then Denise phoned my father, kindly offering him anything of Richard's that he would like. Arthur responded by asking for any Lindner family memorabilia – letters, photographs and so on. Denise said she would send them.

One member of Richard's circle has commented that his widow was overwhelmed by the business of coping with her husband's legacy. Perhaps that explains the fact that she never sent anything. She did phone again, more than once, to tell my father that she hadn't forgotten his request. But he became exasperated by the circularity and fruitlessness of the conversation and, characteristically, ended up telling her what he thought.

Later, in 1986, after Denise's death, Arthur was requested by lawyers to go to London and sign a waiver-and-consent agreement, giving up all rights to his brother's estate, which Denise had left to her sister Anouk. I am not sure what legal advice my parents took. My father was in his eighties by then and had never been interested in anything of Richard's other than the previously requested items that related to their parents. My mother insisted that the lawyers pay for overnight accommodation if he were to make such a trip, and this was agreed to.

He signed the agreement, which was returned to a Madison Avenue law firm. The confirmatory letter states: 'Annette Pappdiamandis [*sic*] has agreed that, to the extent it is within her power, Mr Lindner will be given all family correspondence and family photographs of Mr Lindner's parents located among decedent's effects' after probate.'

That commitment remains unfulfilled to this day.

II

Afterwards

LIVING a largely relative-free life has been my normal. I've observed other people and their circles of grandparents, aunts, uncles, cousins, their long national histories and deep associations of place, and wished, now and then, that I might have known some of those special affections. But on the whole I have not felt personally short-changed. After all, introverts don't do well in large gatherings.

Probably for related reasons, the meaning of family has always perplexed me. My own small group undoubtedly delivered love and affection, but also expectations that I found difficult to fulfil. My mother's perpetual need for reassurance – that her children were alive, that she was a good parent – stunted our relationship. As for boundaries, these felt porous and insecure. The love could be overwhelming, even suffocating. In response to the pressure to live up to Arthur and Else's idea of a good girl I opted to conform, but my internalized half of the bargain was withdrawal – into my own space, physical or mental, and of course, always and still, books.

Family, then, was an isolated place, and I was isolated within it. Where was kinship? Partly in my forceful father, partly in my overlooked, anxious mother, but also partly perhaps in the abstract idea of Richard, in the flickering image of a more clever, more separate, more achieved being. What I have learned about him more recently has only intensified the sense that, warts (and intellectual snobbery) and all, he could have been a role model.

Throughout my life I would bump into his name or his art at unexpected intervals and feel the proud thrill of associated glamour. In 1968, as a student, sitting in some campus lounge one weekend, I opened the *Sunday Times* colour supplement to find a frivolous spread on Pop artists and – could it have been? – their hat stands. Richard was included, his contribution some strange wooden form, head-shaped and rather eloquent, alongside parallel offerings from other, more renowned figures like Andy Warhol.

A few years later, when Penguin decided on a reissue of its Vladimir Nabokov backlist, they selected Lindner reproductions to illustrate the covers. On another occasion, on a business trip to New York, I found myself at a party in the apartment of George Plimpton, editor of the *Paris Review*. There was a Lindner original on the wall. And, as recently as 2014, when Miuccia Prada presented her spring collection, up Richard popped again. 'The clothing was evocative of Richard Lindner's mechanistic cubism,' announced the *New York Times*, with *Vogue* corroborating: 'The work of mid-century artist Richard Lindner seemed to inform the spectacular color-blocking.'[1]

When we met, my uncle and I, in 1967, I believe some kind of bond – part traditional, part more instinctive – was born. But he wasn't a parent, and if he was offering warmth, it would, I discovered, only be on his rather particular terms. The relationship eventually failed because of distance and mis-understanding, perhaps also because of his crankiness and some of my familial uncertainty. Whatever, I regret the lost contact, the opportunity to see his three-dimensionality and to trace what – if anything – there is of him in me. At least the journey of this book has rounded out the portrait of an intermittently charming, occasionally shocking iconoclast, the man whom Priscilla Morgan described as 'sardonic, brilliant, cranky, mean, more an observer than the center of the party, a dominant presence, a serious intellect, a natty dresser, cool, observing, not flirtatious, selfish, vain, with a high opinion of himself'.

And I have heard his voice again in recordings, not so different from my father's – deep, Germanic, linguistically imperfect, but thoughtful, and playful in tone. At least I can now respond to the comment he wrote to me all those years ago – that my parents didn't understand him. The flattering implication was that I did, or at least I have taken it that way. And I think – at least in part – that I do.

Tracing his life has also meant trying to talk about his art through an amateur's comprehension and vocabulary. But it has also required making peace with its content, in particular the women, with their exposed genitalia and brassiness. These Lulus, Valkyries and Amazons are not, of course, to be taken at face value. They are evolving expressions of a philosophy and an experience. They are themselves canvases to which the painter has applied notions of history and society, politics and psychology.

But essentially they make exploitative use of the female form, and additionally they cannot be wholly divorced from the depressing stereotypes applicable to the artist's coterie: the elusive, idealized sister, Lizzy; the dismissed and disparaged mother, Mina; the lost and/or broken first wife, Elsbeth. Lindner's women are fetishized in his art and perhaps were in his relationships, too. If I had been in dialogue with him, would I have dared to challenge him about this?

Richard died four decades ago, and without his supporters his star has declined. But there have been interruptions to that downward trajectory, flares of memory expressed in print, and exhibitions to remind and rekindle. In 1980, for example, Eugène Ionesco wrote a brief appreciation of both Lindner and Steinberg for the magazine *Derrière le miroir*. Steinberg and Ionesco were both Romanian in origin and the playwright had known the artist 'for ages', whereas he 'knew that young man Richard Lindner when he had already passed his three-score and ten'.[2] Ionesco had in fact written the preface to Lindner's final portfolio, published in 1975. Perhaps he sensed kinship in another European iconoclast with whom he shared a focus on the anxieties and social dislocation of the twentieth century. Lindner's *oeuvre* had also been viewed by critics such as Dore Ashton through the prism of drama – the mood of Brecht, the female dominance of Wedekind.

In his brief article, Ionesco compares the style and tone of the two New Yorkers: 'If, for Steinberg, what is comfortable is lined with humour and irony, for Lindner, it is the grotesque in its purest form that is expressed.' The writer found no humour in Lindner's work, and nothing of cubism either: 'Heavy, terrifying, tragic, ugly, caricatures pushed beyond caricature, the world, men are there, heavy and brooding, weighing down the painter. Richard Lindner discovered a kind of genuine beauty in ugliness. What constant trauma. What strength also.'[3]

It's a grim but affecting tribute, and a statement that captures some of Richard's isolation in his vision, and his singular commitment to fulfilling it. Steinberg is the paradoxical romantic of this pair, while Lindner is the paradoxical realist. Steinberg's characters are kept apart thanks to the artist's personal humour. With Lindner, the characters are alone without feeling it, leaving no room for solitude, capable of filling all the space. The juxtaposition is provocative, and extreme. Saul and Richard begin to seem like the odd couple of the visual arts.

Undoubtedly their work diverged greatly, yet their lives and tastes and experiences (and love of cats) overlapped significantly. In notes written after Lindner's death, Steinberg recorded: 'I am still uneasy when talking about Richard as about somebody absent and I realize that I will talk to him – in my mind – the rest of my life. About certain details and associations of ideas known and enjoyed only by us, the only experts.'[4]

In a later statement Steinberg reported on the last two years of his friendship with Richard: 'We spoke on the phone, frequently, about secrets: love, glory, money, desire, and also the mystery of death. The subject was a fitting one for telephonic conversation, there is something posthumous about the phone.'[5] This was their most profound connection: the dark, infinite irony of life, and death.

Towards the end of the twentieth century, there were two solo shows of Lindner's work: one at the Hirshhorn Museum and Sculpture Garden in Washington DC, which moved on to the Haus der Kunst in Munich, in 1996–7, and another at Madrid's Fundación Juan March, which held a retrospective that ran from 1998 to 1999.

I attended both, glad for my uncle that interest still buoyed him up, while feeling marginal to the events, which of course I was. I had visited MoMA in New York some years earlier to ask if they might want to put together any kind of exhibition, and learned there about the activity in Washington. The family was able to make a minor contribution to the Hirshhorn catalogue, in terms of loans of documents and early work. If I hadn't made that initial enquiry in Manhattan, I doubt our branch of the Lindners would have known anything about the preparations or the event itself. The estate had no contact with us. Beyond the grave, the brothers' connection had become ever more attenuated.

In 2009, the George Krevsky Gallery in San Francisco presented Lindner's 'first west coast gallery show in more than 30 years', guest-curated by art historian Peter Selz, who also wrote an accompanying piece for *Art & Antiques* magazine, calling the artist 'significant' and 'unique'. 'No one painted like him.'[6]

And after that... silence?

Not completely. In the virtual world, conversations continue, art markets trade back and forth. If you Google Richard's name, a plethora of galleries, auction sites and institutions pop up. His images spring to life, shocking and dazzlingly coloured once more. To this extent, he is immortal.

One final episode connects me to Richard.

I don't recall why I suddenly began to wonder where he was buried, but when I did, in 2014, it was the work of but a moment to find, online, the answer to the question. The realization that he was nearby, in the posh Jewish cemetery in Hastings, no more than fifteen miles from my current home, arrived with a sense of symmetry, or supernatural coincidence, of a jigsaw piece dropping into place. It was easy enough to drive there one morning, and to follow the instructions supplied at the cemetery office that led me to the actual plot.

The isolation and simplicity of the grave, its hillside location and vista of trees – all this appealed to me. I didn't know Richard hadn't chosen it. It felt as though, if he were going to make his eternal home among the wealthy and talented of his tribe, he would do so on his terms, at a distance. As is customary, I laid a small stone on the slab, and took a photo to show my sister. Then I went home and thought little more about it.

But after a few days, the cemetery's administrator, whom I'd contacted to confirm the grave's location, was back in touch. She had a question. Was I a direct descendant of Richard Lindner? Yes, I told her, my sister and I were Richard's only surviving blood relatives.

Then, she explained, we were the inheritors of the two remaining graves, part of the parcel of three that had been purchased in his name. 'Richard Lindner is currently interred in Grave #2.' Graves one and three were ours, and all monies were paid in full on them.

As unexpected gifts go, this one ranks fairly high in my experience – not something I knew I wanted, but something I rather treasured, now that it was mine. Is this what family feels like, I wondered? Again, I thought the purchase was my uncle's. I didn't believe for a moment he'd made it with my sister and me in mind, but here we were. This, perhaps, was the ultimate in those Christmas boxes he had devoted to us each year of our childhood.

Now I know that it was Denise who purchased the block of three graves, not Richard himself, and my view has altered, has lost its romantic lustre. Richard may have wanted none of it. And why three plots? Splendid isolation, or did Denise intend to be buried with him, and if so, who would take up the other space? Did I want to snuggle up to husband and (notional) wife?

I have no answers to such speculation. But I've decided to take a pragmatic view of this bolt from the blue. Sometimes things just have a way of arriving at an appropriate place or time. Why shouldn't we two American Lindners move in together? In addition, graves cost money and this one – beautiful while to a degree separate – has much to recommend it. I decided to accept the plot, although my sister wishes to rest her bones in the UK and gave hers back.

So Richard and I will spend eternity together. I expect we will both find this grating at times. I need quite as much psychic space as he did. We do though share a taste for cinema and opera, for books and Europe and interesting clothes. We both came of age in the sixties, me actually, he professionally. We have some physical things in common – like diminutive height, and a flat, sloping plane at the back of the skull – and maybe time, rather a lot of it, will allow for a more relaxed exploration of the hinterland that both connects and divides us.

I will be able to tell him more about Arthur, both the good and the bad, and encourage Richard to look a little more kindly on the brother who perhaps, yes, offered more instinct than intellect, more heart than head, but whose reflexes were comparable to some of Richard's own. And I will remind him of my mother's strengths and her loyalty, to counterbalance her wounds and unworldliness. I fantasize this could lead to a more insightful discussion of his own mother, of why he found her so provocative and threatening.

We could discuss the transition from near destitution to financial security, another journey that both brothers had to make in early middle age. In the case of my father, the struggle went on below the surface, concealed beneath a cheery layer of make-do-and-mend. It was, I think, a genuine dimension of Arthur's character, the positive energy to be found in repurposing, in turning rejects into something useful – tools, furniture, even salvaged nails and screws. When money permitted, there would also be low-cost treats: a sudden trip to the cinema; a surprise stop at the fish-and-chip shop. The negative side to all this was a near-obsessive concern that nothing was wasted, certainly not electricity. Hence my own OCD when it comes to the turning off of lights and gas taps, or locking doors. Richard would appear to have had his own narrative about money, and to have struggled longer and harder with the idea of reaching a safe place. Perhaps he had rituals too.

I could spend a lot of time asking my uncle about his first wife and the truth of their time together. Pre-war Paris, filled increasingly with the flotsam and jetsam of European refugees, exhilarating and despairing – what was that really like? Their circle there, the one that fractured into innumerable escape routes during the critical years, then reformed, like mercury, in Manhattan, seems to me a kind of social perfection – friends who offered steadfast loyalty as well as creative and intellectual stimulation, not to mention shared life crises, politics and backgrounds that need no explanation, as well as similar taste in food. Wasn't this the social group I've always sought?

Does it explain my sentimentality towards elderly Jewish gents, the kind featured in Ben Katchor's comic strips of old New York? Or is that just a romanticized view of my father, my uncle and their father, the simpatico Julius whom I never knew?

What about our German-ness, the fingerprint of taint? Mine is second-generation. I never lived there, but visits to the country always leave me feeling compromised, stuck between reflexive familiarity and undying distaste. Richard's identification was bred in the bone. Would that explain his fastidiousness, his immaculate homes where even the notice-boards were arranged with hyper precision? Did he ever cease to feel yoked to the place? He did say to one interviewer, in a conversation about being 'too slow', that 'I don't make it easy for myself. It's a kind of fundamental masochism. The Germans are like that.'[7]

My parents were like that too, not slow or masochistic, but compromised from within. Efforts to scorch away their culture couldn't have been more stringently applied, and my father for one would happily have dumped everything German about himself, and Jewish too, after 1945, for hate and shame. But it wasn't possible. They were hybrids for life and so was our household, my own culture, which came with a 'normal' all its own, a repertoire of phrases, actions, habits that bespoke our otherness:

- Atypical meals, like fried brains (with a squeeze of lemon) for breakfast, or pancakes rolled round green salad for supper in the summer.
- *Dingus* – meaning stuff; *Schnuss* – meaning nose or snout; '*Sie duftet nach falschen*' – meaning heaven knows what, something about making an entrance: funny words and references that I thought my parents had made up, but which turned out to be snippets of other, lost lives.
- Special kits that looked like torture implements. There was the manicure one, stocked with high-quality, precision German scissors, tweezers and the like. Even worse, there was the one for removing splinters – zippered too, made of red leather, which came complete with other, finer tweezers, a loupe and a bottle of potassium permanganate.
- Strange remedies that could seem like witch-doctoring when compared with our neighbours' medical reflexes in Stoke-on-Trent, like the lemon-coloured mohair bonnet my sister or I would have to wear if complaining of earache, after a dose of warm oil had been applied to the offending orifice.
- Peculiar superstitions to do with gloves or knives or the direction in which foam swirled in a cup of coffee.
- My mother's love of roasting whole apples on a toasting fork over an open fire.
- *Und so weiter* (and so on).

In lieu of family heirlooms, or living relatives with memories of earlier generations, these were some of the threads in the fabric of us. They were part of what made us special. But they were also what made us peculiar and separate and I didn't know whether I wholly liked the paraphernalia of otherness or not. If we had to be Jewish, I would think, why couldn't we at least belong to *that tribe*, if not necessarily in terms of faith, then at least as members of a secular bunch with its own network and knowledge bank and humour and educational academies?

Instead, we were stranded in no man's land, familiar with neither Jewish rituals nor English ones, easily wrong-footed by either. Did it hold me back, this groundlessness? No and yes. My life to date has been fortunate, satisfying, stimulating, often unexpected, not short of opportunity. But there's a place, down in the foundation, where it's crumbly, not solid, insecure.

Ironically, now that I live in America, it's assumed I'm British. That's how I sound. My struggles to cope with self-assurance concerning the subject of class are far away and no longer important. The lineage of wealthy Americans is mainly their money. Their snobbery is toxic too, but differently so, and doesn't have the thoroughgoing British power of exclusion. Here I am not intimidated.

And nor was Richard. Here we both encountered a freedom valued and unsought, the byproduct of uninvited change. A gift to us, the last of the Lindners.

Notes

1. THE MEETING

1   Quoted in Werner Spies et al., *Homage to Richard Lindner* (New York: Leon Amiel, 1980), p. 34.

2   *World Journal Tribune* (15 January 1967).

3   Dore Ashton, *Richard Lindner* (New York: Harry N. Abrams, 1969), p. 34.

4   Ibid.

5   Bill DeMain, Gillian G. Gaar and Mike McInnerney, *Sgt. Pepper at Fifty: The Mood, the Look, the Sound, the Legacy of the Beatles' Great Masterpiece* (New York: Union Square/Sterling, 2017), p. 78.

6   George Martin and William Pearson, *Summer of Love: The Making of Sgt. Pepper* (London: Pan, 1995), p. 115.

7   Email correspondence with the author.

8   Quoted in 'Lindner Doll', Peter Nahum at the Leicester Galleries [website], https://www.leicestergalleries.com/browse-artwork-detail/MTQxNjg=.

2. GERMANY 1901–33

1   Dore Ashton, *Richard Lindner* (New York: Harry N. Abrams, 1969), p. 14.

2   'Richard Lindner – American Artist from Nuremberg', Haus der Bayerischen Geschichte [website], https://www.hdbg.de/auswanderung/docs/lindner_bio_e.pdf.

3   'Munich Bans "disrespectful" Holocaust Memorials on Ground', BBC News [website], https://www.bbc.co.uk/news/world-europe-44979359.

4   Werner Spies and Claudia Loyall, *Richard Lindner: Catalogue Raisonné of Paintings, Watercolors and Drawings* (New York and London: Prestel, 1999).

5   Brian O'Doherty, *New York Times* (8 March 1964).

6   Hilton Kramer, *New York Times* (30 April 1978).

7   Judith Zilczer, *Richard Lindner: Paintings and Watercolors 1948–1977* (Washington DC: Hirshhorn Museum; Munich: Prestel, 1997), p. 6.

8   Email correspondence with the author.

9   Ashton, *Richard Lindner*, p. 21.

10   Quoted by John Russell, 'Richard Lindner, Painter Known for Figures of Women, Is Dead', *New York Times* (18 April 1978).

11   Alexandre Alexandre, 'Das Plakat als Kunstwerk', *Das Kunstwerk*, 2/5–6 (1948). Translations from this source are by Monika Carothers.

12 Ashton, *Richard Lindner*, p. 22.
13 Amos Stote, 'Meet Richard Lindner', *Commercial Art and Industry*, 16–17 (May 1934), p. 171.
14 *The Continental Tales of Henry Wadsworth Longfellow*, with drawings by Richard Lindner (Allentown, PA: Story Classics, 1948), p. 128.
15 Ibid., p. 128.
16 Quoted in Madeleine Conway and Nancy Kirk, *The Museum of Modern Art Artists' Cookbook: 155 Recipes: Conversations with Thirty Contemporary Painters and Sculptors* (New York: Museum of Modern Art, 1977), p. 83.
17 Quoted in Werner Spies et al., *Homage to Richard Lindner* (New York: Leon Amiel, 1980), p. 114.
18 Stote, 'Meet Richard Lindner', p. 172.
19 Spies et al., *Homage*, p. 114.

3. FRANCE 1933–41

1 Quoted in Judith Zilczer's notes on Johannes Schaaf's film *Richard Lindner '77* (1977).
2 Quoted ibid.
3 'The Forgotten Camps', JewishGen [website], https://www.jewishgen.org/forgottencamps/.
4 'Camp Esterwegen', Gedenkstätte Esterwegen [website], https://www.gedenkstaette-esterwegen.de/english/#:~:text=Camp%20Esterwegen&text=From%201934%20to%201936%2C%20Heinrich,held%20at%20Sachsenhausen%20onear%20Berlin.
5 Quoted in Werner Spies et al., *Homage to Richard Lindner* (New York: Leon Amiel, 1980), p. 34.
6 Quoted ibid., p. 32.
7 Quoted ibid.
8 Quoted ibid., pp. 35–6.
9 Quoted ibid., p. 36.
10 Larry Rivers, 'A Send-off for Richard Lindner', *Art in America* (November/December 1978).
11 Andrew Hussey, *Paris: The Secret History* (London: Viking, 2006), p. 341.
12 Quoted in Mary McAuliffe, *Paris on the Brink* (Washington DC: Rowman & Littlefield, 2018), pp. 108–9.
13 Ibid., p. 109.
14 Hussey, *Paris*, p. 341.
15 Betty Parsons files, Smithsonian Archives of American Art, Washington DC.
16 Alexandre Alexandre, 'Das Plakat als Kunstwerk', *Das Kunstwerk*, 2/5–6 (1948).
17 Ibid.
18 Ibid.
19 Interview with Colette Roberts, WNYC [radio station] (1965).

20 Alexandre, 'Das Plakat als Kunstwerk'.
21 Quoted in Anne Sebba, *Les Parisiennes* (London: Weidenfeld & Nicolson, 2016), pp. 30–1.
22 Wolfgang Georg Fischer, 'Richard Lindner' [interview], *Art International*, 18/4 (20 April 1974).
23 *The Continental Tales of Henry Wadsworth Longfellow*, with drawings by Richard Lindner (Allentown, PA: Story Classics, 1948), p. 129.
24 Alexandre, 'Das Plakat als Kunstwerk'.

4. UPROOTED

1 *The Continental Tales of Henry Wadsworth Longfellow*, with drawings by Richard Lindner (Allentown, PA: Story Classics, 1948), p. 129.
2 Werner Spies et al., *Homage to Richard Lindner* (New York: Leon Amiel, 1980), p. 125.
3 Ibid.
4 Previously available at http://jewishtraces.org/refugies-france-1939/.
5 Larry Rivers, 'A Send-off for Richard Lindner', *Art in America* (November/December 1978).
6 Meredith Hindley, *Destination Casablanca* (New York: PublicAffairs, 2017), p. 11.
7 Judith Zilczer, *Richard Lindner: Paintings and Watercolors 1948–1977* (Washington DC: Hirshhorn Museum; Munich: Prestel, 1997), p. 16.
8 *Continental Tales*, p. 130.
9 Letter in author's possession.
10 Peter Gillman and Leni Gillman, *Collar the Lot* (London: Quartet, 1980), p. 27.
11 Ibid., p. 43.
12 Benzion Patkin, *The Dunera Internees* (Stanmore, NSW: Cassell Australia, 1979), p. 29.
13 Gillman and Gillman, *Collar the Lot*, p. 245.
14 Ibid., p. 246.
15 Quoted in Cyril Pearl, *The Dunera Scandal* (North Ryde, NSW: Angus & Robertson, 1983), p. 29.
16 Gillman and Gillman, *Collar the Lot*, p. 255.
17 Ibid., p. 249.
18 Quoted ibid., p. 278.

5. ELSBETH

1 'Passengers Come Down Gangway of SS *Siboney* at Jersey City's Harbor and Have Baggage Passed through Customs', Critical Past [website], https://www.criticalpast.com/video/65675074119_SS-Siboney_ship-docks-at-pier_American-Export-Lines_come-down-gangway.

2   See 'Conditions in the French Detention and Internment Camps', Jewish Virtual Library [website], www.jewishvirtuallibrary.org/conditions-in-the-french-detention-and-internment-camps.

3   Meredith Hindley, *Destination Casablanca* (New York: PublicAffairs, 2017), p. 7.

4   Ibid., p. 42.

5   Ibid., p. 53.

6   Ibid., p. 49.

7   'Joseph Bornstein Collection', Center for Jewish History, https://archives.cjh.org/repositories/5/resources/13339. Courtesy of the Leo Baeck Institute, New York.

8   Ibid.

9   Ibid.

10 Quoted in Werner Spies et al., *Homage to Richard Lindner* (New York: Leon Amiel, 1980), p. 114.

11 'Joseph Bornstein Collection'.

12 Ibid.

13 *Mademoiselle* (September 1951).

14 Kesten correspondence (held privately), 7 July 1952.

15 Ibid., 12 September 1952.

16 'Hidden Child in the Netherlands', Holocaust Encyclopedia [website], https://encyclopedia.ushmm.org/content/en/photo/hidden-child-in-the-netherlands.

6. ARRIVAL — 1940

1   *New York City Market Analysis*, compiled by News Syndicate Co., the *New York Times*, the *Daily Mirror* and Hearst Consolidated Publications (1943), p. 2. Available at http://www.1940snewyork.com/.

2   Quoted in Wolfgang Georg Fischer, 'Richard Lindner' [interview], *Art International*, 18/4 (20 April 1974).

3   One of a group of interviews conducted by John Jones for a research project sponsored by the American Council of Learned Societies.

4   Quoted in Johannes Schaaf's film *Richard Lindner '77* (1977).

5   In conversation with the author.

6   *The Continental Tales of Henry Wadsworth Longfellow*, with drawings by Richard Lindner (Allentown, PA: Story Classics, 1948), p. 130.

7   Deirdre Bair, *Saul Steinberg* (New York: Nan Talese/Doubleday, 2012), pp. 84–5.

8   Quoted in 'Charles E. Coughlin', Holocaust Encyclopedia [website], https://encyclopedia.ushmm.org/content/en/article/charles-e-coughlin.

9   Anthony Heilbut, *Exiled in Paradise: German Refugee Artists and Intellectuals in America, from the 1930s to the Present* (New York: Viking, 1983), p. 46.

10 Ibid., p. 46.

11 Ibid., p. 52.
12 Ibid., p. 52.
13 Ibid., pp. 51–2.
14 *Continental Tales*, pp. 130–1.
15 Ibid.
16 George Amberg, 'Richard Lindner', *Graphis* 25 (1949), p. 8.
17 Quoted in Heilbut, *Exiled in Paradise*, p. 141.

7. EVELYN AND THE LETTERS

1 Quoted in 'Hofer, Evelyn', Encyclopedia.com [website], https://www.
   encyclopedia.com/women/encyclopedias-almanacs-transcripts-and-maps/
   hofer-evelyn.
2 Quoted in 'Evelyn Hofer', Galerie m [website], https://www.galerie-m.
   com/artist_info_en.php?aid=65&aname=EvelynHofer.
3 Kesten correspondence, November 1949.

8. THE 1950S

1 Quoted in Judith Zilczer, *Richard Lindner: Paintings and Watercolors 1948–1977*
   (Washington DC: Hirshhorn Museum; Munich: Prestel, 1997), p. 22.
2 Interview with Colette Roberts, WNYC [radio station] (1965).
3 Quoted in Madeleine Conway and Nancy Kirk, *The Museum of Modern Art
   Artists' Cookbook: 155 Recipes: Conversations with Thirty Contemporary Painters
   and Sculptors* (New York: Museum of Modern Art, 1977), p. 95.
4 Grace Lichtenstein, 'Betty Parsons: Still Trying to Find the Creative World
   in Everything', *ARTnews* (March 1979).
5 Deirdre Bair, *Saul Steinberg* (New York: Nan Talese/Doubleday, 2012), p.
   165.
6 Ibid., p. 287.
7 Zilczer, *Richard Lindner: Paintings and Watercolors*, p. 26.
8 Quoted in Dore Ashton, *Richard Lindner* (New York: Harry N. Abrams,
   1969), p. 52.
9 *New York Herald Tribune* (31 January 1954).
10 Betty Parsons files, Smithsonian Archives of American Art, Washington
   DC.
11 Stuart Preston, *New York Times* (22 February 1959).
12 Betty Parsons files.
13 Lee Hall, *Betty Parsons: Artist, Dealer, Collector* (New York: Harry N. Abrams,
   1991), p. 110.
14 One of a group of interviews conducted by John Jones for a research project
   sponsored by the American Council of Learned Societies.

9. THE 1960S

1   Letter to Alison and Peter Smithson, 1957.

2   Werner Spies, introduction to Werner Spies and Claudia Loyall, *Richard Lindner: Catalogue Raisonné of Paintings, Watercolors and Drawings* (New York and London: Prestel, 1999), pp. 9–10.

3   Ibid., p. 9.

4   Stuart Preston, *New York Times* (8 October 1961).

5   Sidney Tillim, *Richard Lindner* (Chicago: William and Noma Copley Foundation, 1961), p. 1.

6   Spies, introduction to Spies and Loyall, *Richard Lindner: Catalogue Raisonné*, p. 9.

7   Tillim, *Richard Lindner*, p. 10.

8   Quoted in *Time* (20 March 1964).

9   One of a group of interviews conducted by John Jones for a research project sponsored by the American Council of Learned Societies.

10 *The Times* (25 June 1962).

11 Thomas B. Hess in *ARTnews*, quoted in Judith Zilczer, *Richard Lindner: Paintings and Watercolors 1948–1977* (Washington DC: Hirshhorn Museum; Munich: Prestel, 1997), p. 31.

12 *Time*, quoted in Zilczer, *Richard Lindner: Paintings and Watercolors*, p. 31.

13 Quoted by the German art critic Hanns Theodor Flemming in *Die Welt*, 1965.

14 Arts Magazine, 1969, quoted in Zilczer, *Richard Lindner: Paintings and Watercolors*, p. 31.

15 Quoted by Flemming, *Die Welt*, 1965.

16 Quoted in 'Lindner Doll', Peter Nahum at the Leicester Galleries [website], https://www.leicestergalleries.com/browse-artwork-detail/MTQxNjg=.

17 George O'Brien, 'Artists' Row', *New York Times* (4 March 1962).

18 *New York Times* (11 August 1968).

19 *Avant Garde*, 1 (January 1968), p. 1.

20 Ibid., pp. 25–32.

21 Quoted in Larry Rivers, 'A Send-off for Richard Lindner', *Art in America* (November/December 1978), p. 149.

22 *San Francisco Sunday Examiner & Chronicle* (22 June 1969).

10. THE 1970S

1   Larry Rivers, 'A Send-off for Richard Lindner', *Art in America* (November/December 1978), p. 151.

2   ARTnow, quoted in Werner Spies and Claudia Loyall, *Richard Lindner: Catalogue Raisonné of Paintings, Watercolors and Drawings* (New York and London: Prestel, 1999), p. 687.

3   Stephen Prokopoff, 'A Conversation with Richard Lindner and Stephen
    Prokopoff', in *Richard Lindner: A Retrospective Exhibition* [exhibition
    catalogue] (Chicago: Museum of Contemporary Art, 1977), p. 22.
4   Quoted in Wolfgang Georg Fischer, 'Richard Lindner' [interview], *Art
    International*, 18/4 (20 April 1974).
5   Quoted ibid.
6   Quoted ibid.
7   Quoted ibid.
8   Parinaud interview, in Judith Zilczer, *Richard Lindner: Paintings and
    Watercolors 1948–1977* (Washington DC: Hirshhorn Museum; Munich:
    Prestel, 1997), p. 33.
9   'Lee Radziwill: Find a New Job', *Vogue* (June 1976).
10 'Richard Lindner', Museum of Contemporary Art Chicago [website],
    www.mcachicago.org/Exhibitions/1977/Richard-Lindner.
11 Prokopoff, 'A Conversation'.
12 *Arts Magazine*, 52 (May 1978).
13 Rivers, 'A Send-off for Richard Lindner'.
14 John Gruen, *The Artist Observed* (Pennington, NJ: A Cappella, 1991),
    p. 90.
15 Ibid., p. 90.
16 Quoted ibid., p. 91.
17 Quoted ibid., p. 91.
18 Quoted ibid., pp. 93–4.
19 Quoted ibid., p. 94.
20 Quoted ibid., p. 95.
21 Letter to Aldo Buzzi, 25 April 1978.
22 John Russell, 'Richard Lindner, Painter Known for Figures of Women, Is
    Dead', *New York Times* (18 April 1978).
23 *Art Now*, April 1972.
24 Hilton Kramer, 'Richard Lindner: Artist of Two Worlds', *New York Times*
    (30 April 1978).
25 Ibid.
26 Ibid.
27 Saul Steinberg Papers, Yale Collection of American Literature, Beinecke
    Rare Book and Manuscript Library.
28 Ibid.
29 Notes given to the author by Nancy Grossman, September 2019.
30 Alexandre Alexandre, 'Richard Lindner 1901–78', *Novum* (July 1978), p.
    54.
31 Ibid.
32 Ibid.
33 Ibid., p. 55.
34 Ibid., p. 54.

II. AFTERWARDS

1   Carolina Irving, Miguel Flores-Vianna and Charlotte Di Carcaci, 'In Living Color', *New York Times* (14 February 2014); Tim Blanks, 'Prada Spring 2014 Ready-to-Wear', *Vogue* (18 September 2013), https://www.vogue.com/fashion-shows/spring-2014-ready-to-wear/prada.

2   Eugène Ionesco, 'Saul Steinberg, Richard Lindner', *Derrière le miroir*, 241 (October 1980), p. 5.

3   Ibid.

4   Saul Steinberg Papers, Yale Collection of American Literature, Beinecke Rare Book and Manuscript Library.

5   Quoted in 'Conversation avec Saul Steinberg', *Repères: Cahiers d'art contemporain*, 30 (1986).

6   Peter Selz, 'Critic's Notebook: A Painter of Modern Life', *Art & Antiques* (2009), https://www.artandantiquesmag.com/critics-notebook-a-painter-of-modern-life/.

7   Quoted in Werner Spies and Claudia Loyall, *Richard Lindner: Catalogue Raisonné of Paintings, Watercolors and Drawings* (New York and London: Prestel, 1999), p. 9.

Bibliography

BOOKS

Ashton, Dore, *Richard Lindner* (New York: Harry N. Abrams, 1969)

Bair, Deirdre, *Saul Steinberg* (New York: Nan Talese/Doubleday, 2012)

Conway, Madeleine, and Nancy Kirk, *The Museum of Modern Art Artists' Cookbook: 155 Recipes: Conversations with Thirty Contemporary Painters and Sculptors* (New York: Museum of Modern Art, 1977)

DeMain, Bill, Gillian G. Gaar and Mike McInnerney, *Sgt. Pepper at Fifty: The Mood, the Look, the Sound, the Legacy of the Beatles' Great Masterpiece* (New York: Union Square/Sterling, 2017)

Gillman, Peter, and Leni Gillman, *Collar the Lot* (London: Quartet, 1980)

Gruen, John, *The Artist Observed* (Pennington, NJ: A Cappella, 1991)

Hall, Lee, *Betty Parsons: Artist, Dealer, Collector* (New York: Harry N. Abrams, 1991)

Heilbut, Anthony, *Exiled in Paradise: German Refugee Artists and Intellectuals in America, from the 1930s to the Present* (New York: Viking, 1983)

Hindley, Meredith, *Destination Casablanca* (New York: PublicAffairs, 2017)

Hussey, Andrew, *Paris: The Secret History* (London: Viking, 2006)

The Continental Tales of Henry Wadsworth Longfellow, with drawings by Richard Lindner (Allentown, PA: Story Classics, 1948)

McAuliffe, Mary, *Paris on the Brink* (Washington DC: Rowman & Littlefield, 2018)

Martin, George, and William Pearson, *Summer of Love: The Making of Sgt. Pepper* (London: Pan, 1995)

Patkin, Benzion, *The Dunera Internees* (Stanmore, NSW: Cassell Australia, 1979)

Pearl, Cyril, *The Dunera Scandal* (North Ryde, NSW: Angus & Robertson, 1983)

Sebba, Anne, *Les Parisiennes* (London: Weidenfeld & Nicolson, 2016)

Tillim, Sidney, *Richard Lindner* (Chicago: William and Noma Copley Foundation, 1961)

Spies, Werner, et al., *Homage to Richard Lindner* (New York: Leon Amiel, 1980)

Spies, Werner, and Claudia Loyall, *Richard Lindner: Catalogue Raisonné of Paintings, Watercolors and Drawings* (New York and London: Prestel, 1999)

Zilczer, Judith, *Richard Lindner: Paintings and Watercolors 1948–1977* (Washington DC: Hirshhorn Museum; Munich: Prestel, 1997)

MAGAZINE AND CATALOGUE ARTICLES

Alexandre, Alexandre, 'Das Plakat als Kunstwerk', *Das Kunstwerk*, 2/5–6 (1948), pp. 26–31

Fischer, Wolfgang Georg, 'Richard Lindner' [interview], *Art International*, 18/4 (20 April 1974), pp. 32–5, 53–7

Ionesco, Eugène, 'Saul Steinberg, Richard Lindner', *Derrière le miroir*, 241 (October 1980)

Mademoiselle (September 1951)

Prokopoff, Stephen, 'A Conversation with Richard Lindner and Stephen Prokopoff', in *Richard Lindner: A Retrospective Exhibition* [exhibition catalogue] (Chicago: Museum of Contemporary Art, 1977)

Rivers, Larry, 'A Send-off for Richard Lindner', *Art in America* (November/December 1978), pp. 146–51

Stote, Amos, 'Meet Richard Lindner', *Commercial Art and Industry*, 16–17 (May 1934), p. 169 ff.

WEBSITES

'Camp Esterwegen', Gedenkstätte Esterwegen, https://www. gedenkstaette-esterwegen.de/english/#:~:text=Camp%20 Esterwegen&text=From%201934%20to%201936%2C%20 Heinrich,held%20at%20Sachsenhausen%20near%20Berlin.

'Conditions in the French Detention and Internment Camps', Jewish Virtual Library, www.jewishvirtuallibrary.org/ conditions-in-the-french-detention-and-internment-camps

'The Forgotten Camps', JewishGen, https://www.jewishgen. org/forgottencamps/

'Hidden Child in the Netherlands', Holocaust Encyclopedia, https://encyclopedia.ushmm.org/content/en/photo/ hidden-child-in-the-netherlands

'Hofer, Evelyn', Encyclopedia.com, https://www.encyclopedia. com/women/encyclopedias-almanacs-transcripts-and-maps/ hofer-evelyn

Jewish Traces, http://jewishtraces.org [no longer available]

'Joseph Bornstein Collection', Center for Jewish History, https://archives.cjh.org/repositories/5/resources/13339

'Lindner Doll', Peter Nahum at the Leicester Galleries, https:// www.leicestergalleries.com/browse-artwork-detail/ MTQxNjg=

'Passengers Come Down Gangway of SS *Siboney* at Jersey City's Harbor and Have Baggage Passed through Customs', Critical Past, https://www.criticalpast.com/video/65675074119_ SS-Siboney_ship-docks-at-pier_American-Export-Lines_ come-down-gangway

'Richard Lindner – American Artist from Nuremberg', Haus der Bayerischen Geschichte, https://www.hdbg.de/auswanderung/docs/lindner_bio_e.pdf

'Richard Lindner', Museum of Contemporary Art Chicago, www.mcachicago.org/Exhibitions/1977/Richard-Lindner

List of Illustrations

BLACK AND WHITE

p. 31   Lindner family group, early twentieth century.

p. 40   Elsbeth Lindner teaching, late 1920s or early 1930s.

p. 70   The box Arthur made.

p. 75   Elsbeth Lindner.

p. 129 Richard Lindner in photographer Evelyn Hofer's studio, 1950, with *Verlaine* and *Proust* portraits and *Anna (Woman in Corset)* in the background. Photo by Hermann Landshoff, location Münchner Stadtmuseum, Munich. Art Resource, NY.

p. 134 Richard Lindner with his VW, New York, 1957. Copyright Estate of Evelyn Hofer.

p. 141 Arthur, Else and Elsbeth, Chester Zoo, 1950s.

p. 170 Richard and Denise Lindner, New York, 1960/70s. Copyright Estate of Evelyn Hofer.

p. 200 Richard Lindner's gravestone at Westchester Hills Cemetery, Hastings-on-Hudson, NY.

COLOUR PAGES

1. *a)* *Offenbach* by Richard Lindner. Photo by John Kempsey.
   b) One of the famed Barnes piano adverts.
2. *The Meeting* by Richard Lindner, 1953, copyright Museum of Modern Art (MoMA), New York, USA, Licensed by Scala, Florence.
3. *Ice* by Richard Lindner, 1966, copyright Whitney Museum of American Art, New York, Licensed by Scala, Art Resource, NY.
4. Crayon drawing by Richard Lindner for his niece Elsbeth.

Acknowledgements

Many people have assisted me in this project and I am grateful to all these individuals for their generosity.

Rebecca Aldi
Michael and Stefan Bornstein
Alison Burns
Kevin Clark
Bill DeMain
Mary Ellis
Jean-Pierre Fenie
Dagmar Friedrich
Jonathan Galassi
Ernesto Giraldez
John Githens
Nancy Grossman
Jann Haworth
Les Hudswell
Mary Ingham
Madeleine and John Kempsey
Richard Lehfeldt
Peter Nahum
Steven Novelli
Andreas Pauly
Nancy Schwartz
Sophie Sequeira
The late Irene Skolnick

Hildegard Thevs
Judith Zilczer

The following institutions also offered invaluable assistance.

American Academy of Arts and Sciences
Beinecke Rare Book and Manuscript Library
The New School, New York
Hedda Sterne Archive
Saul Steinberg Archive
The Morgan Library, New York
The Smithsonian, Washington DC
The Center for Jewish History
New York Public Library
The Solomon R. Guggenheim Museum
Hirshhorn Museum and Sculpture Garden, Smithsonian
    Institution, Washington DC
The Department of Homeland Security Genealogy Program,
    US Citizenship and Immigration Services
The MoMA Archive
Betty Parsons Archive, Smithsonian Archives of American Art